My Personal Pentecost

W9-BHR-920

My Personal Pentecost

Edited by
Roy S. and Martha Koch

Foreword by Kevin Ranaghan

HERALD PRESS
Scottdale, Pennsylvania
Kitchener, Ontario

Except where otherwise indicated, Scripture quotations are from the King James Version or from the Revised Standard Version of the Bible, copyrighted 1946, 1952, © 1971, 1973.

MY PERSONAL PENTECOST
Copyright © 1977 by Herald Press, Scottdale, Pa. 15683
   Published simultaneously in Canada by Herald Press,
   Kitchener, Ont. N2G 4M5
Library of Congress Catalog Card Number: 77-79229
International Standard Book Number: 0-8361-1816-2
Printed in the United States of America
Design: Alice B. Shetler

DEDICATION

We lovingly dedicate this book
to our children and grandchildren
who give us much joy and inspiration.

CONTENTS

ACKNOWLEDGMENTS

We are happy to acknowledge our indebtedness to the writers of the testimonies in this book for their willingness to report their failures, false starts, and then their blessings as they entered into the deeper life of the Spirit. Their openness has given their words the ring of authenticity.

Several other individuals also come to mind who gave encouragement and helpful advice in the preparation of this book. Nelson Litwiller, retired missionary, statesman, and world traveler, was most helpful in his encouragement. R. Herbert Minnich, chairman of Mennonite Renewal Services and his wife, Shirley, who also serves on the committee, prayed with us many times over this work and rejoiced with us in its completion. Dr. Kevin Ranaghan, former president of Catholic Renewal Services and now director of the National Communication Office serving the Catholic Charismatic Renewal, read the manuscript and graciously consented to write the Foreword of the book.

Finally, we express our deep appreciation to Paul M. Schrock, book editor of Herald Press, for guiding this book through the intricacies of publication and for giving many valuable suggestions to enhance its effectiveness.

FOREWORD

We are living at a unique moment in the history of the church. Something is taking place in divided Christianity which is genuinely new. God is moving simultaneously in all the Christian churches, pouring out the same gifts and graces of the Holy Spirit.

It is not surprising that Christians should experience renewal and revival. But that the same grace of renewal should touch all the churches at once and bear the same spiritual fruit and have the same life-changing results is remarkable. This is a reality in today's Christianity increasingly permeated with charismatic renewal, the "New Pentecostalism." Baptists, Lutherans, United Methodists, Presbyterians, Catholics, Episcopalians, Brethren, Orthodox . . . the list goes on and on.

In each church and denomination there is this swelling of personal commitment to Jesus Christ our Lord and Savior. In each there is a growing acknowledgment that Christians, to be effective disciples of the Lord, need to be radically dependent on the presence and power of the Holy Spirit. In each there is a renewal of prayer, of listening to the Word of God, of holiness, and of deeper commitment among brothers and sisters in Christ. In each there is the experience that Christian ministry and discipleship are empowered from on high.

Today there is a breakthrough of the supernatural power of the risen Lord—His liberating, transforming, healing, delivering ministry—through the humble service of the members of His body. All of this is happening in every denomination and around the world today.

This book is about this renewal as it is being experienced by Mennonites. It is a touching, stirring book. In broad strokes and in fine detail it recounts how God has touched, healed, blessed, and reshaped the lives of men and women who in all sincerity and openness sought Him in His fullness. The situations are highly varied, the people decidedly different from one another. All are Mennonites, yet their backgrounds, ages, ministries, needs, and dispositions cover a broad spectrum. In each case there is the discovery of the constant love of the Father through the blood of Jesus in the many manifestations of the power of the Holy Spirit.

The writers speak more personally than "professionally," even though many of them obviously come from years of outstanding Christian ministry. For the reader with questions and concerns regarding the hows and whys of this Mennonite spiritual renewal, Roy Koch's introduction is especially helpful.

Personally this book is a great joy to me. I first came into serious contact with Mennonites as a theology student at the University of Notre Dame. I was already deeply involved in the charismatic renewal in the Catholic Church when I began to study Anabaptist history and theology under Dr. John Howard Yoder. I gained a deep respect for the convictions, principles, worship, holiness, and service of these newly discovered brethren. Subsequently through the fellowship of Nelson and Ada Litwiller I came to know of the thousands of Mennonites who today are enjoying the same spiritual renewal that has blessed my family.

Now in this book readers can share my happiness in the vitality of Mennonite life today within the context of the worldwide outpouring of the Holy Spirit in all churches.

Kevin Ranaghan
Charismatic Renewal Services
South Bend, Indiana

INTRODUCTION: THE BAPTISM WITH THE HOLY SPIRIT

Roy S. Koch

The "New Pentecostalism" that has been sweeping the Christian world in the last two decades has compelled many staid, conservative denominations to engage in some fresh studies on the subject of the Holy Spirit and the renewed life. That something fresh has been happening to persons who have long been faithful Christians is beyond doubt.

What term to use to describe this new vitality in the churches has not been determined with finality. The most commonly used designations are the "baptism in the Holy Spirit" or the "baptism with the Holy Spirit" or the "baptism of the Holy Spirit." The proper preposition to use with the term is a matter of dispute with many Christians.

Some denominations steer clear of the term altogether preferring to call it a "release of the Spirit." One highly respected theologian, J. Rodman Williams, president of Melodyland School of Theology in Anaheim, California, prefers to call it the "Pentecostal reality." Other writers identify the whole movement with the term *glossolalia* which is Greek for speaking in tongues. Others reject glossolalia because it emphasizes only one aspect of the gifts of the Spirit, that of speaking in tongues, when in fact there are many gifts of the Spirit.

One description that seems to be as acceptable as any of this new stir in the churches is "charismatic renewal." But there are some who do not relish this term either. I have no vested interest in any given term and prefer that the reader use whichever description seems suitable to him.

The writers of the testimonies in this book describe a great variety of experiences. We hope that the reading of these accounts will convey clearly at least this much, that something authentic and blessed has happened to them.

I consider myself a rather typical Christian as regards the charismatic movement. I think I see plainly three stages in Christian circles on this subject. The first stage may be called *Abomination*. This is the stage when we ridiculed the whole movement and considered those caught up in it as more or less lunatic. We loved to tell stories of their far out antics. The "holy rollers" of those early days got scant sympathy from us. This abomination stage in the history of the churches lasted a long time and still clings on in some places.

The second stage in the church might be called *Toleration*. This stage dates back to the Sixties, or possibly into the Fifties. This was the stage when we began to be a bit more respectful of the whole movement. It is also the time when the "New Pentecostalism" was finding acceptance in many other denominations including the Roman Catholic Church.

I recall how I discovered that respected pastors and prominent laymen in whom I had great confidence claimed to have received the baptism with the Holy

Spirit. But I failed to be really turned on until the Sixties. I remember the cumulative effect all these testimonies had on me. I could not in good conscience deny the reality of their experiences, yet my whole background predisposed me against them.

Finally, in desperation, I sought the Lord in earnest prayer. I pleaded for some token of His guidance. The first Sunday after my heartfelt prayer, one of our church members at the South Union Church in Ohio invited me to accompany him to a Full Gospel Business Men's dinner at Columbus, Ohio. The invitation was more than mere coincidence, of that I was convinced. I interpreted it as guidance from God.

I must confess that I had some fears about attending the dinner because I knew that the FGBM's organization was unabashedly charismatic. I was afraid that some of my fellow church members might see me at the dinner. After all, I was active in our church organization as bishop of the South West Ohio churches and had served as moderator of our district conference. In fact, I served one term as moderator of Mennonite General Conference. Would I jeopardize my reputation by being seen at such a dinner? So I went with some trepidation. As feared, I was recognized by some Mennonites there, but they welcomed me with open arms.

That evening I heard a message in tongues for the first time in my life. The entire group had their heads bowed in prayer while the message was being given. I was there to soak up all I could, so I peeked. After all, didn't Jesus say we are to "watch and pray"?

I was so impressed with the genuineness of the testimonies and the warmth of the fellowship that I told

Martha, my wife, "You must by all means attend one of these meetings." That was the real beginning of our involvement in the charismatic movement.

The stage of toleration gradually gave way to the third stage in many circles, *Propagation.* The soft-spoken charismatics gradually found their voices and began to give their testimonies without fear. The Seventies are seeing Holy Spirit Consultations, Festivals, and Renewal conferences from one end of the Christian church to the other. Both religious and secular magazines carry articles and reports of charismatic renewals. Some people are happy with this development and some are not.

In my own experience, I have read dozens of books and articles on this fresh work of the Holy Spirit in our time. I have learned the names of outstanding men and women in many denominations like Kathryn Kuhlman, Sam Shoemaker, Dennis Bennett, Russell Bixler, Larry Christenson, J. Rodman Williams, Don Basham, John Sherrill, David du Plessis, Kevin and Dorothy Ranaghan, Nelson Litwiller, and dozens of others.

I am frankly impressed by these testimonies of spiritual reality and renewal. I still have some unanswered questions and some disagreements with what I consider as extreme emphases in doctrine, but I do not intend to reject what is manifestly a work of God because of a few aberrations.

I have had to become accustomed to a cultural pattern considerably different from my upbringing. I refer to uplifted hands in praise, applauding in worship services, closed eyes, and happy smiles on upturned faces.

Why should we discuss this subject now and risk alienating good friends? It is a good question. Why rock the boat when we are sailing along so smoothly? But is our "sailing along" quite as smooth as we pretend? Problems in our churches and in our nation have been multiplying so fast that we cannot seem to keep up with them. The old answers are no longer good enough for tensions in families, the generation gap, divorce and broken homes, and a rapidly rising crime rate all around us.

On the other hand, we see fresh vitality in churches that have experienced this new movement of the Spirit. Young people hooked on drugs find deliverance and get turned on to Jesus. Older Christians whose lives were jaded and marked with a lack of spiritual interest suddenly blossom out into enthusiastic Christian workers. A new reality marks the worship services, money is released for the cause of Christ, and the level of spiritual life leaps upward.

We should at least acquaint ourselves with what is happening in this "New Pentecostalism." Moreover, if it is as good as it appears, should we not open ourselves to the same kind of newness? If it has done so much for others, could it do as much for us? What can happen in our churches if we lay aside our old prejudices and let this "wind of the Spirit" blow through our congregations? We should not castigate this new movement as mere emotionalism and then dismiss it without further examination.

But why should this burst of renewal come upon us now? Others have asked this question. Who is wise enough to interpret God's timing? Some have called this renewal the "latter rain" when God's sovereign Spirit begins to move to call His people to Himself. It is not for us to question God nor to apologize for the past. Our part is to respond to the movement of the Spirit of God in our time.

A Brief History of the Charismatic Movement

Many scholars take us back to the day of Pentecost (Acts 2) as the origin of the baptism with the Holy Spirit. Actually, however, there are a number of foregleams of Pentecost in the Old Testament.

Michael Harper, in his book *Power for the Body of Christ*, sees "the root of it in the Old Testament, the stem or trunk in the Gospels, and the flower or fruits in the Acts of the Apostles and the Epistles."[1]

An amazing incident is reported in Numbers 11. Here, in desperation, Moses slaps his resignation on God's desk and declares emphatically that he is through leading God's people. God sympathetically instructs Moses to name seventy elders of the people upon whom He will place His Holy Spirit and thus enable them to share Moses' load. This infilling of the Holy Spirit apparently was the solution to the problem.

Jeremiah talks of the new covenant that God will make with the house of Israel and the house of Judah (Jeremiah 31:31-33). Ezekiel speaks of the gift of a new heart and a new spirit and of God putting His Spirit within His people (Ezekiel 36:25-27). Isaiah speaks of God's Spirit upon the Messiah (Isaiah 42:1; 61:1) and upon the people (44:3; 32:15). Perhaps the most dramatic Old Testament Scripture is found in Joel where God promises to pour His Spirit upon all flesh (Joel 2:28, 29).

Let us bypass, for the moment, the Holy Spirit's renewing ministry in the New Testament and trace something of the Spirit's ministry throughout the church age. The charismatic gifts have never completely died out in the church. They have always been present, but they have blazed up into public view during times of revival and spiritual renewal.

The *Encyclopaedia Britannica* states that glossolalia "recurs in Christian revivals of every age, *e.g.* among the Mendicant friars of the thirteenth century, among the Jansenists and early Quakers, the converts of Wesley and Whitefield, the persecuted Protestants of the Covennes and the Irvingites."[2]

In the second century AD, Montanus became disillusioned with the spiritual coldness of the church and sparked a revival during which time all the charismatic gifts appeared. Tertullian and Iraneus, two notable church fathers, were very favorably impressed for a time. Eventually the church officials in Rome declared Montanus a heretic because he departed from the accepted Scriptures in the course of time.

The Irvingites of the nineteenth century, followers of Edward Irving, a Presbyterian pastor in London, England, also practiced the charismatic gifts. Among his followers a new denomination was formed known as the Catholic Apostolic. Larry Christenson, in his book *A Message to the Charismatic Movement*,[3] takes this denomination as something of a model for today.

The Pentecostal Movement in the United States had its beginning in 1900 at Topeka, Kansas. The first person to speak in tongues did so on New Year's Eve, 1900. From this slow beginning the revival spread to California in 1906. Azusa Street in Los Angeles has become famous as the locale of a Pentecostal revival lasting for three years with thousands of people from all over North America receiving the baptism with the Holy Spirit. In fifty years Pentecostal membership climbed to nearly ten million.[4]

Today this Holy Spirit revival has overflowed the Pentecostal Church and has become what is popularly known as the "New Pentecostalism" taking in most of the Christian denominations. Episcopalians, Presbyterians, Roman Catholics, Lutherans, Baptists, Methodists, Mennonites, and many others bear testimony to the fact that they have experienced the baptism with the Holy Spirit.

The early Pentecostals who experienced this baptism tended to come mostly from the semiskilled or unskilled people. Today some of the most outstanding intellectual and professional people claim this experience or speak approvingly of it. As examples, permit me to name Samuel Shoemaker, deceased Episcopalian leader of Pittsburgh; Dr. James I. McCord, president of Princeton Theological Seminary; Dr. Ernest Wright of Harvard; Bishop Leslie Newbigin, former president of the World Council of Churches; Dr. Van Dusen, former president of Union Theological Seminary in New York; Kevin and Dorothy Ranaghan of St. Mary's College, South Bend; and many others. For quotes from some of these leaders I refer you to *They Speak with Other Tongues*,[5] and *A Handbook on Holy Spirit Baptism*.[6]

Some denominations are putting forth a resolute effort to keep this "heresy" out of their ranks. I am not at all optimistic about their chances of success. I believe that this movement is an open door provided by God and no man can shut it.

What the Baptism of the Holy Spirit Does Not Mean

Some charismatic leaders may not agree with me on the points that follow, but from what I have read and observed and experienced I have arrived at these conclusions:

I do not believe that a person is unsaved unless he has the baptism with the Holy Spirit (as understood in this special way). The baptism is for Christians only. I believe it is possible, perhaps altogether too common, that persons have the gracious experience of the new birth but lack the fullness of power and blessing that the baptism confers. We shall have occasion to refer to this later.

I do not believe that a person does not have the Holy Spirit unless he has the "baptism" with the Holy Spirit. We cannot be saved without receiving the Holy Spirit.

I do not believe that the baptism is glossolalia oriented, or that we must speak in tongues else we do not have the baptism. Here I part company with those who make that assertion. I prefer not to call the charismatic movement "glossolalia" because it directs the attention to only one of many Spirit-given gifts. Moreover glossolalia has a somewhat uncomplimentary connotation.

I do not believe that to claim the baptism with the Holy Spirit means to overemphasize the Holy Spirit. This *can* happen with some it is true, but it is not an essential part of the baptism experience. My observation is that the whole movement exalts our Lord Jesus Christ to His rightful place in our lives.

I do not believe that the baptism experience minimizes loyalty to the Scriptures. I believe the very opposite is true. If a person has a liberal theology, it brings him back to a new loyalty to the Word of God. On the other hand,

if a person has a wooden and legalistic interpretation of
the Bible, it may well demolish that kind of biblicism.
Persons who have experienced the Spirit baptism, or
infilling, develop a new loyalty and love of the Word.
You will see this truth referred to again and again in the
testimonies in this book.

I do not believe that the baptism with the Holy Spirit
makes us schismatic. This charge has been leveled at
charismatics for a long time. In some cases it may be
true, but more often such people are "pushed out" of
their fellowships. I have seen this happen. The strong
tendency is for charismatics to become truly ecumenical,
loving and enjoying fellowship with spiritual people of
all denominations.

I do not believe that the baptism is a purely subjective
experience and results in an abandonment of social issues
and proper ethics. Not for a minute do I wish to deny the
subjectivity of the experience, but to claim that a good
feeling is all there is to it, is to be blind to its reality.

What Does the Baptism with the Holy Spirit Mean?

Here we come to the crux of the matter. A wide reading of books shows both similarity and dissimilarity of
meaning. Don Basham says very directly and freely,
"The baptism of the Holy Spirit is a second encounter
with God (the first is conversion) in which the Christian
begins to receive the supernatural power of the Holy
Spirit into his life. . . . This second experience of the
power of God, which we call the baptism in the Holy
Spirit is given for the purpose of equipping the Christian
with God's power for service.[7] Many, but not all charismatics, will agree with Basham.

Many people find themselves uncomfortable with the term "baptism of the Holy Spirit." Some, who may agree with Basham on a second experience, prefer to use other terms and reserve the term "baptism" for the conversion experience.

Various terms are used to describe the baptism with the Holy Spirit. These are "baptism," "falling upon," "pouring out," "receiving," "being filled," "giving," "renewing," and "anointing." Read these terms in Acts 2, 8, 10, 11, 19; Luke 11; Titus 3; and 1 John 2.

The experience of the "baptism" is actually a loose term and is called by all the aforementioned words to indicate the "original" experience of receiving the Holy Spirit. Apparently the baptism of the Holy Spirit can be called by any of the above terms. Is it then possible that we make too much of an issue if we disallow the term "baptism" for any experience with the Holy Spirit subsequent to His first or original filling of our lives?

Whatever term is used, the experience is the same. It establishes a fresh, dynamic relationship between the Christians and the Lord.

But what is the experience of the baptism itself? Is it indeed a "second encounter with God"? A "once for all" event in the church's experience? A sort of cosmic shove to get things rolling? Most charismatics believe that the baptism with the Holy Spirit recurs in every generation of Christians that opens itself to it. Just as there were successive outpourings in the early church, they continue even now. Charismatics claim with some biblical justification that the promise of the Holy Spirit is to the children of the children's children of all who call upon God.

Charismatics do not deny repeated fillings of the Holy Spirit, but they believe that the baptism with the Spirit is something different. Spirit baptism is an anointing from God that confers supernatural power, praise, supernatural gifts, and a new boldness to witness for Jesus. Not to be confused with gradual sanctification, it is a decisive act of God. At least some charismatics make a distinction between the reception of the Holy Spirit at conversion and the later filling of the Spirit.

The baptism by one Spirit whereby we are all baptized into the body of Christ (1 Corinthians 12:13) is the action *of* the Holy Spirit placing us into the Christian church. The baptism *in* the Holy Spirit, on the other hand, is Christ's work through which He places the Holy Spirit upon us and within us in a baptism of power for service.

It is at this precise point that theological differences become manifest. If the charismatics are correct in their interpretation, then there is biblical justification for the experience that many claim. It may also be fair to say that the only point on which charismatics themselves agree doctrinally is that they confess to having experienced a personal Pentecost. Beyond that one experience lies a great variety of doctrinal opinion.

We may well ask, "How does this baptism come to us?" I have sat at scholarly consultations as this topic was discussed. I am convinced that scholarship alone cannot lead us into this experience. Scholarship must be the handmaid of obedience and faith as we contemplate Jesus Christ and the Holy Spirit.

Many theologians insist that experience must always be subject to the corrective of biblical doctrine. There is much truth to this claim, but there comes a time, too, that doctrine and theology must be subject to the corrective of experience. Take for instance the controversy about circumcision that erupted in the apostolic church. The Jerusalem theologians knew of no way whereby uncircumcised Gentiles could enter the Christian church. They had Scripture upon Scripture that declared emphatically the need of circumcision to belong to the people of God.

Yet Paul and Barnabas brought to the Jerusalem Conference Titus, an uncircumcised Gentile Christian (Acts 15, Galatians 2) who was Exhibit A that God accepted a believing Gentile into His family without circumcision. Out in the mission field of Syria were hundreds more like Titus. It was imperative that apostolic theology make room for this "experience" that countered their theology.

What was the result at Jerusalem? Theology was modified so this new phenomenon could be included in it. This modification of theology was not permitted to become an exception to the rule but became the norm in the practice of the early church.

Some teach that all the fruit and gifts of the Spirit are inherent in our conversion experience which is all the baptism there is. Whatever we receive later is a fuller realization of what we already have and is not an additional work of God. The baptism, so called, comes to us upon our acceptance of the lordship of Christ. Those who receive what they call the "baptism in the Spirit" have been ignorant of their experience or have never before made Jesus Christ Lord of their lives.

I am deeply impressed with this view and agree with much of it, but it does not agree with my own experience.

There are many others who say the same thing about their experience. I had consciously made Jesus Lord in my life years ago. Theoretically, I should have had the "baptism with the Holy Spirit" at that time. But it was not until I specifically asked for the Holy Spirit anointing (baptism, release, freedom, or whatever) that I received a fresh experience of joy, release, and power. Must I now repudiate my experience so I can harmonize it with this particular view of theology? Let us not deny the reality we have experienced.

Both Williams and Christenson have some keen observations on this point. Williams says, "The person of Pentecostal experience does not begin with a theology about the Holy Spirit, not even a biblical teaching as such, but with something that has happened in his life. . . . Baptism, filling, gift, reception. . . . though biblical, are not primarily understood by exegeting certain texts. Rather, these terms are helpful ways of defining what has occurred."[8]

Christenson observes that "there is a sound theology for the baptism with the Holy Spirit. But the baptism with the Holy Spirit is not a theology to be discussed and analyzed. It is an experience one enters into.[9]

These quotations sound like putting the cart before the horse. If one wants to nag about this it is possible, but doesn't New Testament practice bear out both men's claims? In every experience of Holy Spirit baptism recorded in the Book of Acts, the experience preceded the theology or explanation of it.

Let us now examine a number of New Testament texts to see whether the baptism with the Holy Spirit initiated the new birth experience or followed upon it. Can the baptism with the Spirit be separated from conversion?

It is altogether fitting to begin with Jesus Himself. He was conceived by the Holy Spirit, born without a fallen nature, and lived a perfect life. But Jesus did no miracle, nor did He manifest unusual powers until He was baptized with the Holy Spirit. His baptism is described in Luke 3:21, 22. A particular part of His baptism by John was the baptism by the Holy Spirit.

Immediately after the Holy Spirit baptism, Jesus demonstrated Holy Spirit power in His ministry. Notice particularly Luke 4:1 and then 4:14, 18, 19. "Full of the Holy Spirit, Jesus returned from the Jordan, and for forty days was led by the Spirit up and down the wilderness and tempted by the devil. . . . Then Jesus, armed with the power of the Spirit, returned to Galilee; and reports about him spread through the whole countryside. He taught in their synagogues and all men sang his praises. . . . He opened the scroll and found the passage which says, 'The spirit of the Lord is upon me because he has anointed me; he has sent me to announce good news to the poor, to proclaim release for prisoners and recovery of sight for the blind; to let the broken victims go free, to proclaim the year of the Lord's favour' " (vv. 1, 14, 17-19, NEB).

Even in the Son of God there was a dynamic change when He had received the Spirit's baptism. In His entire ministry Jesus demonstrated all the gifts of the Spirit with the possible exception of tongues and their interpretation.

In Luke 11:11-14 Jesus instructed His hearers to ask the Father for the Holy Spirit. Were these unsaved persons or saved persons who were to make this request?

Obviously saved. When the Holy Spirit baptized the 120 at Pentecost, did He baptize unsaved or saved? Apparently the latter. These examples are taken, of course, from the transition period between the Old and the New Testaments and so should not be treated as the norm for all time.

Let us move on to the Samaritans as recorded in Acts 8. There is no question here about their salvation nor as to whether they lived in the Christian era or not. They were converted by the power of the Holy Spirit, but *they did not have the baptism of the Spirit.* According to the theology of many people this simply could not happen, but it did. This development in Samaria was considered so abnormal that the Jerusalem church sent Peter and John down to them to complete their experience by ministering the Holy Spirit to them. Not for a moment did they consider the Samaritan experience good enough and leave it alone.

In the house of Cornelius, conversion and Holy Spirit baptism were simultaneous, but it was not always so. In Paul's case he was converted on the Damascus Road and was baptized with the Holy Spirit three days later.

In Acts 19 we have the story of the twelve men from Ephesus who were disciples of John the Baptist and did not have the Holy Spirit. Paul ministered the Spirit to them. Notice the question he asked them, "Did you receive the Holy Spirit when you believed?" Why should he ask that question if there were no possibility of separating the two experiences? The answer is obvious, there is a possibility of being born again by the power of the Holy Spirit without receiving the *baptism* of the Holy Spirit.

Apparently Timothy received the Spirit's baptism some time after his conversion when Paul and the church elders laid their hands on him (1 Timothy 4, 2 Timothy 1:6). The conclusion seems inescapable, the Holy Spirit baptism may *or may not* be experienced at conversion.

The Results of Holy Spirit Baptism

This is an exciting topic. The twelve men of Ephesus are something of a parable with meaning for today. How many times could Christians in our churches be asked, "Did you receive the Holy Spirit when you were converted?" Why this question? Because of a manifest lack of joy and praise and power. Isn't there more power and joy than most of us demonstrate? Must we go through life with an experience deficient in power and reality?

How aptly Williams describes such powerless communities! "The believing community may still be existing without the actualization of its potential. This is not to deny that such a community is the people of God, called into being by His Word and Spirit, and living by His grace . . . but the release may not yet have occurred where the Spirit from 'on high' and from within moves mightily to actualize the vast potential. The Christian community, despite the fact that the new has come, may not yet have entered upon the fullness of what is available. Latently it is all there, but it has not yet come to manifestation. The situation thus is one laden with vast possibility, but the 'happening' whereby it takes on dynamic vitality may not have occurred. The explosive power has yet to break loose." [10]

It is true beyond the shadow of a doubt that many

Christians live far below their potential. I have had even
ministers and missionaries sit down and talk to me, with
discouragement and fear, of their frustrations with problems that are beyond solution. We need a new infusion of
power, we need a ministry of deliverance.

If we are too weak and powerless to cope with the
situation facing us in our churches, is the solution to add
more staff, or perchance to increase our efforts? The
experience of Moses in Numbers 11 is instructive at this
point of our need. It was not the *number* of people who
could help him most but the *quality* of their experience.
When God's Spirit came upon them they received the
enabling that solved the problem.

When this anointing of the Holy Spirit breaks into our
lives and churches there is power and release. There is
something "additional" to our creeds and forms. Salvation becomes vivid, there is an awesome delight in God.
It is as though the shekinah glory has returned to the
tabernacle. Our community of faith takes on a new and
exciting meaning. There is a thrill in reading the Word, a
continuing mood of praise, thanksgiving, and joy. Love is
released, our possessions are available to God for His
service, and there is a new sense of freedom in our worship. The gifts of the Spirit become operative as we encourage one another. Persons bound in sin and defeat
find deliverance. Miracles of knowledge, wisdom, and
healing become evident. Many persons find a prayer language that revitalizes their worship of God.

One such anointed person said, "There is an awareness
of having entered a vast new spiritual realm." Another
one said, "It was like being flooded with joy." Still
another commented, "With me there was peace. Just a

wonderful, quiet, steady, deep peace."[11]

Kevin Ranaghan described the experience in these words: "All the characteristics of Christ we have read about in the Epistle to the Galatians (5:22, 23) and which we have sought—the love of Christ, mutual forbearance and concern, the lack of strife and contention within community—these become tangible and real through the baptism in the Holy Spirit. It can be like a foretaste of heaven."[12]

How Does One Receive the Baptism of the Holy Spirit?

This question brings us to the vital issue confronting us. If this is an experience we all need, and if there is a shade of possibility that God has more for us than we now possess, then let us by all means find the means of achieving this experience.

I hope that none of us shall be like the Anglican minister who at 75 admitted that he had been living on the wrong side of Pentecost all his life. Finally he swallowed his pride, prayed for the baptism with the Spirit, and discovered the power that satisfied him as never before.

"Only one thing seems to be essential; an authentic request that is radical, open, and available to the answer that the Lord will send."[13]

Williams suggests that an attitude of openness and expectancy is helpful. At one point he mentions four things that should characterize us: (1) an openness, (2) a yearning, (3) a willingness to be ministered to [it is humiliating for a minister to admit to such need and have others lay hands on him], (4) a growing sense of need in the church.[14]

In the Book of Acts the Holy Spirit was given suddenly and without forethought (Acts 10). He was given at times in response to the laying on of hands (Acts 8, 9, 19, 2 Timothy 1:6). The pattern obviously varies. God responds to the desires of the heart and is not limited by outward forms.

It is helpful to create settings where this experience can happen which reflect openness, acceptance, and expectation. There should be a request for the gift, then a response of praise to God in the faith that He has done as He promised.

Let us not be afraid of the gifts of the Spirit. Let us seek them for ourselves and for others. May God pour upon us and upon our brothers and sisters the renewal of the Holy Spirit. Let Him restore to us the shekinah glory, the radiance and glow that is the heritage of His people. May we create in our families and among our friends such a climate that no one shall be embarrassed to seek for the baptism and the gifts of the Spirit.

Conclusion

Some time ago I found a quote that I treasure: "This is project No. 1 for all Christians—the unrestrained, unhindered, controlling presence of the Holy Spirit in our lives—to allow the power of God to fall upon and live through His people." [15]

Stephen B. Clark said, "If it is a true body of Christ, each member should experience the presence of the Spirit in his life and the whole community should experience all the charismatic gifts (including tongues, prophecy, healing, miracles, etc.)" [16]

There is still much to explore on this subject, but I

prefer to let it be said by those who have opened their souls to this experience and are willing to tell us about it. Their accounts follow in this book. You will see that their experiences vary greatly. No one can set forth a set of rules that the Holy Spirit must follow. The Spirit is free, He blows where He wills. Nevertheless some common experiences seem to characterize most of them.

> Spirit of the living God, fall afresh on me;
> Spirit of the living God, fall afresh on me.
> Melt me, mold me, fill me, use me,
> Spirit of the living God, fall afresh on me.

1. Michael Harper, *Power for the Body of Christ* (Plainfield, N.J.: Logos, 1970). p. 16

2. Eleventh edition, Vol. 27, pp. 9, 10.

3. Larry Christenson, *A Message to the Charismatic Movement* (Minneapolis, Minn.: Bethany Fellowship, 1972).

4. Don Basham, *A Handbook on Holy Spirit Baptism* (Springdale, Pa.: Whitaker House, 1969), pp. 5, 6.

5. John J. Sherrill, *They Speak with Other Tongues* (New York: Pyramid, 1965), pp. 64-66.

6. Basham, *op. cit.*, pp. 7-10.

7. *Ibid.*, p. 10.

8. J. Rodman Williams, *The Pentecostal Reality: The Charismatic*

Renewal Put in Theological and Historical Perspective (Plainfield, N.J.: Logos, 1973), pp. 17, 18.

9. Christenson, *op. cit.*, p. 40.

10. J. Rodman Williams, *The Era of the Spirit: Barth, Brunner, Tillich, and Bultmann on the Holy Spirit* (Plainfield, N.J.: Logos, 1971), p. 54.

11. Sherrill, *op. cit.*, p. 113.

12. Kevin and Dorothy Ranaghan, *As the Spirit Leads Us* (Paramus, N.J.: Paulist Press, 1971).

13. *Ibid.*, p. 12.

14. Williams, *The Era of the Spirit, op. cit.*, pp. 36, 37.

15. H. S. Vigeveno, *The Early Church Speaks to Us* (Glendale, Calif.: Regal Books, 1970), p. 7.

16. Ranaghan, *op. cit.*, p. 34.

MY PERSONAL
PENTECOST

1

CAPTURED BY THE GENUINE

Robert and Lois Witmer

The Counterfeit Healer

"Can you come home for a day or two? Some wonderful things are taking place," the letter from Robert's sister implored. "This man has a real gift from God, yet he's so humble about it. He's a medical doctor and a physiotherapist, and he's going on in psychiatry. He says there's so much he doesn't understand, he's just learning. He just believes. When the power comes over him and his left hand gets real hot, he gives a treatment.

"He has healed many around us. A neighbor girl was blind in one eye and now she can see. Her grandfather was almost deaf, after one treatment he can hear. Others have been healed of cancer, polio, diabetes, and heart disease. He removes kidney stones and gall bladder stones without surgery.

"We couldn't believe it, but when you watch him you just have to marvel! He says his doubting Thomases always become his best disciples! Do you think you could

---

Robert and Lois Witmer from Ontario have been missionaries in France since 1956. They work closely with the French Mennonite Mission, of which Robert is executive secretary, in providing a Christian witness among foreign students who come to Paris to study.

come? Perhaps he could heal your eyes."

We were shocked! The family was taken in! What should we do? It was November 1955. We were in Goshen, Indiana, for my last year of seminary training. It was Saturday noon. The letter was sent from our home in Ontario on Thursday. Was the man still in our home?

We conferred. We prayed. We checked out our convictions about going home with one of our professors in the seminary. He agreed, suggesting that the first thing we do is put the man out of the house then call in several ministers to help straighten out all who may have become involved. "But you've got a hot potato on your hands," the professor cautioned. We could feel it!

Everyone was up when we arrived home early Sunday morning. Dr. Ford himself appeared shortly in the kitchen. He had gone to bed only a few hours before. We greeted him and began asking questions about his family, his medical training, his certificates, his church affiliations, his understanding of the gospel, and of his special gift of healing.

After an hour or so, while he went outside to light a cigarette, we had a few minutes to talk alone with the family. We saw several "patches" covering running sores, a large kidney stone in a little jar, and several badly infected "tailbones" in another jar. Under no circumstances was anyone to touch any of these. Dr. Ford himself would touch them only with his left hand.

When he came back into the house we asked him if we could watch him give treatments. "Certainly," he said "I do everything openly."

"And if we would take X-rays before and after, would that be all right?"

"I have hundreds of them at home," he replied.

At the breakfast table when we began talking about the morning church service, he became very "pious" and wondered whether it might be possible for him to take communion. He had never met Mennonites before, it was only by accident that he got to know us through the neighbors with whom he was staying. Sensing that the family was increasingly on our side, we became more daring in our questioning. "If you left here, where would you go? Did you register when you came here?"

"With the police you mean?"

"Yeah, do they know you're around?"

"No, I hadn't thought of it."

"You wouldn't mind if we gave them a call and let them know you're here?"

"Not if that's what you want to do." Soon, having gone outside for another smoke, he disappeared, leaving his belongings behind.

That afternoon we had a doctor examine the "running sores." They were second-degree burns that had formed big blisters and were now draining. In Dr. Ford's suitcase were various "miracle helps" that could produce burns, and many coloring powders. The police were quite interested in the assortment. Two weeks earlier they had been on his trail after a man filed charges concerning a diabetic cousin's sudden death. But all the witnesses had nothing but praise for Dr. Ford.

The next ten days, while Dr. Ford was awaiting trial, our family received protests of every description. "How can you who claim to be Christian people say anything bad about this wonderful man of God? I was actually dead, and he brought me back to life!"

Skepticism Increased

Back in seminary and for a long time afterward we harbored strong feelings about miracle-working "faith"
healers! We welcomed openly the many stories that were
circulating at the time such as someone watching a healing service behind the stage. Five men walk in. One lies
on the stretcher. Later in the evening the other four carry
the "lifetime invalid" onto the platform. The evangelist
lays hands on him and shouts, "Give glory to God. Stand
on your feet. Now run around the auditorium!" And he
does! The crowd becomes almost hoarse! Or of a family
traveling to a big crusade who stop at a restaurant for an
early supper. That evening at the meeting they are
shocked to see the waitress in agony on crutches. In sympathy they ask what happened and she whispers, "Shh, I
get paid well for this!" We have never had opportunity
to gather evidence to substantiate these reports but they
satisfied our feelings at the time.

The medical reports on experiments where half of a
group of ill persons received a new wonder drug and the
other half unknowingly received "identical" sugar pills
also held our attention. The healings reported among
those who received only sugar pills but believed they
were receiving the newly discovered remedy, confirmed
the great psychological effects of "faith" in physical
healing.

Vaccinated Against the Charismatic.

The "vaccinating effect" of these experiences, as well
as reports of the many exaggerations and aberrations in
certain Pentecostal circles, were certainly not a great
asset in preparing us to open ourselves to the so-called

charismatic dimension of Christian experience. The teaching we had received concerning the periods of miracles in the Bible corresponding to the periods of divine revelation throughout the history of God's people made sense to us.

No need to question the authenticity of miracles in Bible times, we thought. But now that the revelation is complete in Christ Jesus we no longer need the confirmation of miracles. Likewise, now that Pentecost has fully come—not only to the Jews (Acts 2) but also to the Samaritans (Acts 8) and to the "uttermost parts" (Acts 10) —the specific manifestations accompanying His coming had also fulfilled their purpose. To expect such manifestations to be repeated should be outside the scope of our expectations, we reasoned.

A Fruitful Ministry, but—

Our first fourteen years of missionary experience were not without challenge and blessing. The Holy Spirit was at work in our lives and through our ministry. We believed and taught that life under the lordship of Jesus Christ means life in the Spirit, without whom our efforts would be futile. There were "seasons" of Spirit-fruit bearing. Certain natural gifts committed to the Lord became, we believed, gifts of the Spirit to the church. We would in no way wish to discredit what was truly of the Lord in our ministry throughout those fourteen years.

Yet we were not satisfied. Were we allowing the Lord to do all that He wanted to do in us and through us? The "living water" did not seem to flow as a river out of our hearts (John 7:38, 39). We clearly understood that anyone who thirsts should come to Jesus to drink. We

thirsted. We came to Jesus. But where was the river? Dry
sands were blowing too often. We looked for streams in
the desert! Now and again we came to an oasis. Testimonies of springs were circulating in books from various
circles by other men and women of God. Their careful
biblical interpretation opened a crack through which the
Spirit began to manifest Himself more fully to us.

In October 1969 Robert became seriously ill. A biopsy
to obtain a bone specimen for examination confirmed the
diagnosis as plasma cell cytoma, a form of bone cancer. It
was a time of deep soul searching. We prayed! We
trusted in God. We shared with the family and with the
brotherhood. We requested anointing with oil, according
to James 5:14-16. We read books such as *The Healing
Light* by Agnes Sanford. The Lord intervened!° While
continuing to return regularly for tests during these past
seven years Robert has to date received no treatment of
any kind for plasma cell cytoma.

The Lord was good indeed! What was He trying to tell
us? Miracles did no doubt serve as signs to confirm special revelation throughout the history of God's people.
But did not Jesus act also primarily out of love and compassion for a suffering people?

We continued to thirst during the months that
followed. Several new books and articles stimulated our
expectancy of what God had in store for us. Were the
spirit's manifestations really to be limited only to the
initial stages of kingdom extension as a sign-confirmation
of His coming? Or should the rivers still be flowing?

°Robert Baker, *God Healed Me* (Scottdale: Herald Press, 1974),
pp. 74-78.

The Well Flows Again

In November 1970 a retired missionary visiting missions in Europe spent two nights and a day with us. We were eager to know whether reports we had heard about charismatic renewal in both Catholic and Protestant circles were well founded. To our surprise our dear brother bubbled with enthusiasm as he shared his own experiences. For years on the mission field he had struggled against Catholics on the one hand and had despised Pentecostals on the other. Two opposite poles! Then he heard of Catholics receiving the Holy Spirit. He wondered what a Catholic Pentecostal looked like. He went to see. He thirsted. He drank. Something happened! And he hasn't been the same since! "But I'm still so young in the experience. I wouldn't know how to help anyone," he told us.

We pondered. Sleep was sporadic. We waited on God. Next morning before breakfast we asked the brother if it really mattered that he was still so young in this new experience. Would he pray with us anyway?

With hands on our heads, he first praised God for His completed work of salvation in Jesus Christ. Proclaiming the lordship of Christ he commanded with authority that all powers of evil, as agents of Satan, withdraw from us in defeat, and that our whole being be cleansed. Then he asked Jesus, the Spirit-baptizer, to release His Spirit in us.

It was like opening the shutters of the bedroom window on a bright sunny morning! The triune God has not changed, but He added a new dimension to our relationship with Him. Liberation made love, joy, and peace something more than pious concepts. Deliverance from the power of evil, and freedom in the Spirit, began to take on new significance in human relationships.

It has been a growing experience over these past six years. We have become increasingly conscious of the weakness of our own spirit and of the power of His Spirit. Ministering in the name of Jesus to bring healing, deliverance, wholeness, comfort, and fullness to those who seek and submit to Him has added much joy to our service for Christ. It does not happen automatically nor independently of the will of those we serve—neither in their initial experience nor in their continuing walk in the Spirit. Together as we live and walk in Spirit community, the reality of the body of Christ in peoplehood relationships becomes progressively more meaningful. Indeed, the Spirit does not do for us what He expects us to do for ourselves, but how different than trying to do it alone!

What about doctrinal formulations and the wider church fellowship? We have always been concerned about avoiding polarization of opinions and positions. By all means the true work of the Spirit is not divisive! Just as we understand the Holy Spirit to act in perfect "gentlemanly" fashion, doing violence to no one, so we believe we must be patient and tolerant.

While we stand ready to indicate the Source of living water for all who thirst, we do not feel compelled to seek to prove a more adequate doctrinal statement of the relation between regeneration and the baptism in the Spirit. This latter point seems to be the major stumbling block for many evangelical leaders here in France who quite readily rejoice about the charismatic renewal in Catholic and Protestant circles but can fit it into their own doctrinal position only on the level of regeneration. Therefore, many evangelicals are still dusting desert sands while Catholic and Reformed groups, who ostensibly need doctrinal correction (!) on various points, are drinking deeply.

Our negative experiences with fake healer Ford twenty years ago not only made us wary of phoniness during our own time of searching. It has continued to keep us alert to what could be simply manifestations of psychological, emotional, or sensational stimulation. Indeed, we have needed to repent of the exaggerated questioning shadows we cast on all purported supernatural manifestations over a number of years. Because of our limited perceptiveness and fear of aberration, we may well have quenched the Spirit on various occasions even in recent years.

We need to keep a balance. We need to exercise the Spirit-directed gift of discernment to differentiate between the Spirit and spirits. Indeed, the majority of cases we meet are not as blatant as the crafty Dr. Ford. All the more reason to be alert. We need each other's Spirit-guided counsel. Truth bears examination. The examiners will not stumble if they are openly committed to the Spirit of truth.

We rejoice in praise to God for the wholesome attitude within our brotherhood and for the freedom with which the Spirit is working to bring renewal to many.

2

THE HOLY SPIRIT IS MAKING US ONE

Donna and Charles Hensler

Dear Charlie,

Twenty-seven years have passed since we repeated our vows of commitment to each other. "And these two shall become one flesh," the minister read. Yes, we have been "one flesh," and we are increasingly becoming one Spirit.

Our spiritual growth was sporadic and quite erratic, wasn't it, Charlie? First you had a surge of spiritual growth and I lagged behind. Then several years later the Christian life became really exciting to me and I moved ahead, thinking that I needed to be the spiritual leader of our family. I was wrong. Charlie, forgive me.

I know that if we had been communicating on a deeper level, you would have come through. Thank God, later on we were able to do that, and now we are walking hand in hand, keeping pace with each other. One Spirit!

Donna and Charles Hensler of Kokomo, Indiana, are active in the Marriage Encounter Movement. Charles is a heating and air conditioning contractor and Donna is a staff chaplain at St. Joseph Hospital in Kokomo. Both hold leadership positions in the Parkview Mennonite Church, Kokomo.

My Priorities Were Wrong

I'm still in the process of becoming, but a few special experiences have changed my life. I remember back to 1966. Our children were 11, 13, and 15. I was working as a Red Cross volunteer in our local hospital. You were a successful businessman. We had a nice home, many friends, and were quite active in our local church and church related activities. I had everything, yes, even more than I could have ever wanted in life. Yet I still felt unfilled.

I sensed that there must surely be more to the Christian life than I was experiencing. There must be a missing link that I had not discovered. I recall that one Sunday morning in Sunday school class when I was very critical. I said, "Let's stop playing church and get down to business in our Christian lives." But I didn't know what direction to go.

My priorities were misplaced. Decorating our home in the latest color scheme, planning and sewing a fashionable color-coordinated wardrobe for myself and our daughters, and making sure that the men in our family always looked topnotch—these matters of appearance were so very important to me. God was somewhere down at the bottom of my list.

The Spirit of God Awakened Me

About this time our church community became involved in Bible studies. In small groups we shared our interpretation of the Scriptures and how the Scriptures affected our personal lifestyles. Here was meaning. Here were close, caring relationships with other Christians. This was the church.

An unquenchable thirst for the knowledge of God caused me to read many, many books in our church library. I kept searching for something more.

One Sunday our minister shared with our congregation his newfound joy in the Holy Spirit. He related a physical healing he experienced and shared his excitement of the Spirit-filled life. As I listened with the ears of my soul, I knew, at last I knew, this is what I had been searching for. This was the missing link, the something more, the Spirit of Christ. I began to read books about the Holy Spirit and His rightful place in the trinity. He had always been a mystery an unknown to me. I was amazed to find the Scriptures full of references to the Holy Spirit. As I continued to read more and more, the New Testament seemed to come alive.

It Was a Baptism of Love

Late one night, after reading John Sherrill's book, *They Speak with Other Tongues,* I knelt by the hearth of our fireplace and asked God to baptize me with His Holy Spirit. After thanking and praising Him for all He was to me, I dared to allow words to come from my lips which I did not understand. I felt no self-consciousness, Charlie, only a lifting of my spirit to His.

Suddenly I heard myself singing words I did not understand to the tune of "My Jesus I Love Thee." I experienced a release of my spirit to Christ that I had never known before. Tears started flowing—tears like I had never cried before. The floodgates of my inner being were opened and an ocean of tears washed away my doubts, my fears, my loneliness, and my emptiness. Then a calm surrounded me—a silence heard only in the middle of the night. And I knew I was at one with God.

I recalled the story of Peter wanting to erect three shelters on the Mount of Transfiguration, so he could stop time and hold on to the glory he had experienced.

Growth Comes by Sharing

One of my first thoughts the next morning was, "What will Charlie say if I tell him about my beautiful experience of a prayer language?" Because of my mistrust of your acceptance, I didn't tell you for several months. Forgive me, Charlie, for not sharing my experience with you. I'm sure we both missed a blessing because of my hesitancy.

Part of my reluctance to share my newfound joy was the strong feeling in our community against the new movement of the Holy Spirit. Some thought speaking in tongues must be of the devil. Others said that only an unstable person would need to speak in tongues. There was a general mistrust of anyone involved in the charismatic movement.

I shared my new experience with only a few persons at first. These persons were a great encouragement to me. Yet in less than two weeks, I started doubting all that happened. Only as I went back again and again to the Word of God's love did I know that the experience was genuine—God's gift to me.

One morning after you had gone to work, Charlie, and the children were in school, I sat in our living room reading, praying, asking God to minister to my doubts and fears of unreality in my Christian life. I was just waiting on the Lord. I remembered Rosalind Rinker sharing her experience of letting the Lord speak to her through her own voice. I said, "Lord use my voice, please." I waited.

I suppose I expected Him to start talking without effort on my part. Yet I know He uses our wills. So I started in, "Donna, my child," and the words began to flow. "I love you. I have created you different from any other person. You have gifts, but you seem afraid to use them. My child, I love you; I love you." By this time I was weeping. Then I sensed His hands on my head saying, "I baptize you with love."

That experience changed my life. Although we have gone through many valley experiences since then, Charlie, I have never felt afraid or alone.

I thank God that as I honestly began to share with you my spiritual pilgrimage, we started to grow together. We had been one in flesh, but we are becoming one in Spirit. Thank God.

Your constant love and respect have been my anchor, Charlie. I love you.

Donna

Dear Donna,

Your life has been a real witness to me. You say you didn't tell me of your spiritual experience, as if we only communicate by words. In fact, I doubt if you could live with me without betraying that God was working in new ways in your life. You dropped many clues—the way you responded to the family, the interest you took in spiritual things, the reading you did, your increasing concern about others. Yes, Donna, you told me without words and I began to like what you were saying.

As I read your experience of receiving God's Spirit I am impressed with how different it is from mine. Yet I am convinced that the Spirit of God is struggling within me too to fashion me into what He wants me to become, and to work out His will in my life.

I received the Spirit of God through several types of experiences. For me it wasn't a one-night happening but rather a continuation of events since my conversion. Many times I felt far from God before I learned to trust Him completely and depend on His Spirit to lead in my life.

Repentance Makes Forgiveness Real

I noticed that every time I would repent and confess sin in my life peace and inner joy engulfed my being. I think of the time I took something from a factory and had to go back and make it right. I can still remember the feeling I had upon leaving the building. Tears of joy trickled down my cheek. For the first time in a long while I seemed to be able to reach God in prayer again.

My most recent experience caused me a lot of frustration until I finally realized God was trying to get my attention. Praise God, He finally got through to me.

Four or five months ago I discovered a physical problem in myself. It was not too serious, but it seemed to hang on and on, so I went to the hospital for tests and X-rays. After extensive tests that all proved negative, I finally realized my physical problem was caused by a personal relationship that I had found hard to deal with. Only after confronting that person and sharing my wrong feelings did I find emotional, physical, and spiritual healing.

Donna, after all the times I've hurt other people, regardless of how unintentional it was, I still find it hard to realize the importance of repenting in order for spiritual healing to take place. But repent I must if God's Spirit is to be alive in me.

The Word Nourishes My Spirit

Another way I notice Christ's Spirit struggling to come alive in me is through His Word.

I haven't always been faithful in reading and searching the Bible to see what God wants to tell me day by day. I realize that by my unfaithfulness I have been cheating myself of some of God's richest blessings. But those special times when I have had a real hunger for the Word have been climactic in my spiritual experience. It has changed my life to read the Bible from cover to cover, or to read it by topics, or by chapters. At those times I have sensed God living and working within me and giving me His person.

Recently I received a special blessing by reading the epistles that have a lot to say about the Holy Spirit—Galatians, Ephesians, and Romans. As I read Galatians several times in different translations, the work of the Holy Spirit became increasingly important in my life. I was fascinated to discover that God gives His Spirit only when we believe in Christ and trust Him fully and ask the Spirit to come into our lives. The Holy Spirit enables me to believe and trust! I began to become conscious of what kind of Spirit He is. For the first time in my life I realized that it is more important that I have the right Spirit than it is for me to be skillful in communication. If I have the Holy Spirit, He will convict me of the evil things I do as a human being.

When I meditated on the fruit of the Spirit—love, joy,

peace, and the like—and to what degree I had them, I sensed that the Spirit still has a lot of work to do with me. It was exciting for me to learn that God the Father has sealed me by the Spirit. It felt so good to know that I belonged to God. His Spirit has sealed me as His very own. Praise the Lord!

Reading the Word became increasingly exciting. It seemed to me that when I was Word-filled I was also Spirit-filled, I felt powerless when I neglected to read the Word. I need your encouragement in this area, Donna.

A Caring Fellowship Builds Us Up

I appreciate so much the fellowship and caring of other Christians. Sometimes I think, "Oh, well, who cares anyway?" I've had to ask God's forgiveness for thinking that way because I've really been affirmed by others many times. Sometime ago I was injured in an explosion and had to be rushed to the hospital. Word traveled fast through our community that I was hurt. A week or two later I discovered that many people were concerned. People would stop me and tell me how their church or group were praying for me. It feels so good to know that people really care. How wonderful to be a member of the family of God!

I thank God for fellow Christians who encourage me. My Spirit-filled friends have been a great help to me.

Donna, I could not close without telling you how much it means to me for you to be Christ-serving and Spirit-filled. Our days together are growing better, and I am convinced it is because of our relationship with Christ and His indwelling presence. I will always love you.

Charlie

3

GOD'S WAYS ARE HIGHER THAN OUR WAYS

James Delp

I stood in the corner of the basement, tears running down my face. A sense of joy filled my heart. I was overwhelmed by the presence of the Holy Spirit. What this experience meant, I really didn't know. One thing was certain. I had met my Lord in a real and personal way.

What were the circumstances behind this experience? What had caused me to climb off that scaffold as I had begun my day as a carpenter subcontractor working on new homes in Columbia, Maryland?

To put it simply, I had finally surrendered to Jesus and was reaching out for all He had for me. Too long had I given only brief, pat answers and failed to meet the heart cries of our struggling brothers and sisters in Jesus.

My Call to Preach

During the month of July 1970 I was visited by the

James and Janie Delp grew up on farms in Lancaster County, Pennsylvania. Since 1962 they have lived in Baltimore, Maryland, where James worked as a carpenter for several years. He has pastored the Baltimore Mennonite Mission and has been active as a Mennonite evangelist.

leaders of my congregation. I was not aware of the purpose of their visit. It came as a complete surprise when they informed me that the Lord had spoken to them that they should ask me to serve temporarily as pastor of the congregation I was attending in Baltimore City. I was to begin in several weeks when our former pastor would be leaving to attend school.

Being a good Mennonite and being a preacher were two different things as far as I was concerned. In the thirty years of my life I had learned a few things about my Lord and how He dealt with mankind. One important lesson I had learned was that when He presents you with an opportunity you'd better take it seriously and be certain of His will before you answer those He used to present you with that opportunity.

After praying about the matter a few days and still not having a clear sense of direction, my wife and I asked the Lord to speak through a situation. He gave us an affirmative yes and I began to wonder if He knew what He was doing.

Several weeks later, I stood facing my congregation at the end of my first sermon with notes lying before me that represented weeks of frustrating study. I groped for more words but none came. I was embarrassed because I knew the truth was open before everyone. I couldn't preach. I felt sorry for myself and more sorry for my people. How would I ever get through this situation of having to be a pastor for several months?

The next sermon was no better but as I prayed fervently and studied the Word, I began to see before me a choice. I could go on in my miserable condition trying to fulfill my calling with my abilities in the flesh, or I

could surrender all to Jesus and trust Him to empower
me to be the person He wanted me to be.

My hypocritical life was revealed to me as I had never
seen it before. I was enmeshed in materialism. I was
selfish. I did not have my heart in the mission work but
only used it as a front for my hypocrisy.

At first I justified my weaknesses and refused to call
them sins. As I studied the Word I realized that God's
children were to be happy and joyous in their callings,
but I was a miserable, sad preacher. If I was to survive,
God would have to do something for me.

God Is at Wits' End Corner

I had made new commitments before, only to fail
when the Lord asked me to carry out all the details involved. This time I had to go all the way. I was at the end
of myself. I could not go on in my miserable condition. I
poured it all out to my Savior the best I knew how. That
same week, I found myself reading from 1 Corinthians 12
concerning the gifts of the Spirit. The big commentary
which I had just bought told me that the gift of prophecy
is sometimes interpreted as the gift of preaching.
Something about that statement caught my attention.
Wasn't it logical that if I was called to preach, my Lord
would give me this gift? I had never asked for any gifts
before, but I had never realized how great the Christian
life was supposed to be. I simply asked my heavenly
Father to give me this gift. Whether I was a temporary
preacher or not, I needed it.

Nothing unusual happened until I stood up to preach
the following Sunday. This was my third or fourth
sermon. I began to preach without really trying very

hard. I experienced a new freedom and a new power. I didn't understand what had happened. I didn't know that God had anointed me to preach the gospel. Every Sunday I would ask my heavenly Father to do it again, and He would. After doing this about fifty times, I realized what had happened and thanked Him for what He had done and would continue to do for me as long as I was faithful to Him.

As I continued to experience this new adventure, the Lord began to reveal areas of my life He wanted to clean up. I had to confess to my congregation the sin of gossiping about them. I had to make restitution for some property I had damaged twelve years before. The Lord showed me He was not pleased with the use I was making of the sense of humor He had given me. I loved to tell jokes, and for years had done almost anything for a good laugh. I was afraid life would become sour without a lot of jokes to keep things loosened up. When I surrendered my sense of humor to God, the Lord gave me a message that not only gives happiness for a few minutes but lasting joy and peace to others forever and ever. Hallelujah.

But God Had Still More for Me

I soon became aware of an additional need in my everyday life. I had emptied out all of self and God was blessing my life. He had anointed me to preach, yet I did not have the daily freedom and power that I sensed I needed to live for Jesus. My congregation still needed a better leader. My wife needed a better husband. My children needed a better father. I groped for the answer to this need.

I had heard a few times about the baptism of the Holy

Spirit, but it was not clear to me what it was all about. There were no prayer and praise groups around that I knew of. But I knew that God would meet this need in my life when I was ready.

Many times during my youth when I was tempted to stray or faced a rough experience, I would read the account in the gospels of the suffering and death of the Lord Jesus. This would always encourage me to go on. Again I was led to read and meditate on Calvary but this time it was not just an account of Jesus' suffering and death. It became an experience with personal dimensions to me.

For two or three days I could not think seriously about anything else. Constantly a mental picture of the horrible torture and death of the Lord Jesus loomed before me. I was overwhelmed by it. I grasped the fact as never before that this was for me personally. I no longer needed to sense guilt for past sins. The price had been paid for Jim Delp's old nature and I no longer needed to respond to it. It was dead, and when it tried to come alive it could be conquered by the same Spirit that brought back to life the body of the Lord Jesus and now lived in me. Hallelujah.

As I tried to begin my work that spring morning, the experience I was having at the cross became too much to keep under control on a scaffold fifteen feet off the ground. I went into the house that I was working on and wept tears of joy. The emptiness was gone completely. I had the assurance that I could do and be whatever my personal heavenly Father wanted and expected me to be. I had nothing to fear, for now I was more than a conqueror through Him who loved me.

Many new things began to happen. After that it was difficult to act like a normal person. All I felt like doing was praising the Lord.

About a year later, as I was reading material concerning baptism of the Holy Spirit, the Lord revealed to me what my experience was all about. This discovery was a blessing because many times after it took place, I asked to have the same experience again. I now understood that it was just the beginning of the Spirit-filled life. If I wanted to stay filled, I would have to continue to let the glory flow through me and out to others or I would become filled with sin and self again.

God Is Sufficient in the Valley of Sorrow

Since then I have had to learn many lessons in humility and to undergo many severe testings. The severest test of all began on June 24, 1972, the week of Hurricane Agnes. This was also the day before I was ordained to the ministry, for now I was to become a permanent preacher. I am limited in this writing to share the many important details of this experience which climaxed on December 17, 1973.

My oldest son, Jerry, then nine years old, was diagnosed as having leukemia. From the beginning of this experience to the end we learned to walk in the Spirit. Many times the Lord touched Jerry when hands were laid on him. He lived a rather normal life during most of his illness. As we sought the face of God continually, He seemed to assure us that Jerry would be healed physically. Many signs pointed to this.

During a time of desperate prayer for Jerry my wife, Jane, received the baptism. I also was completely healed of a gall bladder condition that had afflicted me for twelve years.

We lived in anticipation of the day Jerry would be completely healed. I began to travel as an evangelist. Everywhere I went I shared openly what I believed concerning my son's healing.

Jerry was an unusual boy for his age. His constant desire was to please Jesus. We marveled at the faith he demonstrated at such a young age.

In the fall of 1973 his condition worsened. We still hung on in faith. We made every serious decision on our knees believing God for complete healing. The last thing that could be done for him medically was to perform a bone marrow transplant using his sister's bone marrow which matched his perfectly. The Lord showed us we should go ahead with this. The transplant was performed and in a few weeks it looked like a success. All blood cells came back clear of leukemia. The blood count was up to normal. Everything on the charts looked great.

Everyone was praising the Lord, for we understood from the doctors that what was learned from Jerry's experience could help many leukemia patients in the future. But a few complications set in from the transplant which left Jerry feeling bad.

On December 15 Jerry looked at us and said, "Mommy and Daddy, I have to tell you something. Last summer I was thinking about heaven and about Jesus and I decided I don't want to be healed. I want to go to be with Jesus." I didn't take it seriously for I knew he was feeling badly that day. Two days later, as his mother sat at his bedside holding his hand and talking about Jesus, he left us.

It startled me. Where was God? What did this mean? I cried for him to come back. But in a few minutes I grasped the reality that my son was in the presence of Jesus. It was just his earthly house lying before me. Never again would he see a needle or have to take a drug. His spirit was no longer suffering because of his physical body. He was completely and gloriously healed. It was what he had wanted.

Doctors, friends, and others were also startled by his death. We all had been so sure of his physical healing. We had failed to realize that God deals with individuals and even at the age of 10 a little boy could walk so close with Jesus that no one, regardless of their faith, could interfere with what he and Jesus had decided on.

As I write these lines almost two years later I must be honest and say that I still am tempted to become depressed, for I had many plans for my son. But each sorrowing experience ends with joy and gladness as I am overwhelmed with the fact that my son walks with Jesus.

Had we not known what it meant to be filled with the Spirit, we would probably have fallen apart over this experience. But we had the confidence through it all that the Lord was leading.

Now we can praise the Lord and claim the victory over a situation that Satan intended to cause our defeat. Because of it, our lives have become richer, my messages more authentic, and I have a greater ability to get people to look up, for their redemption draws nigh.

The most important thing for any Spirit-filled person to do is to take time to walk slowly and humbly before God and man, continually letting His glory roll out in praise and blessing to the Lord Jesus and never forgetting that we are more than conquerors through Him who loves us.

It is my desire that these few lines may strengthen, uplift, and encourage some struggling saint and most of all bring honor, glory, and praise to my precious Lord and Savior, Jesus Christ.

4

THE COLLEGE COED WHO STRUCK IT BIG

Sharon Martin

My Turmoil Gave Way to Peace

I knew as I rode home from church that night that something wonderful had happened. There was something different about my parents and about this man, John Smucker, who was to be the special preacher at our church for the following week. What happened to them? What was it that made them seem so different? I had heard the altar call in the Sunday morning, afternoon, and evening services. I knew God was working in our church and miracles were happening. People were praising God like I had never heard before.

Was this a revival? What possessed these usually stable, Christian people of our church at Poole?

I knew that I was a Christian and had accepted Christ but I also knew God was calling me. I wanted so much to be a part of what was happening, but was I ready? I felt so unworthy, so afraid of what God might ask me to do. I

Sharon Martin of Milverton, Ontario, has studied early childhood education at Conestoga College in Kitchener. She is a member of the Poole Mennonite Church where her father, Amsey Martin, is the pastor. She is employed at Anne Hathaway Day Care Centre in Stratford, Ontario.

was also uncomfortable and restless. If you've ever heard the call of God and not obeyed, you'll know what I mean.

I heard my parents talking in the front seat of our car, and for some reason tears began streaming down my face. I couldn't stop crying, but I didn't know why. I tried to hide my tears and blow my nose quietly. Never before was I so glad to get home and be alone.

At this point I wasn't too sure if I wanted to go to any more of Smucker's meetings. The next day at school I couldn't think of anything except wondering what was going to happen in the meeting that night. It was a long and frustrating day for me.

Well, eight o'clock finally rolled around and the service started. John stood at the front and talked with force, but gently and beautifully. He preached without notes and just seemed to be talking with us. The audience was really quiet and reverent. I knew before he finished that this was the night I was going to make a new commitment. In fact, I could hardly wait for him to finish his message.

The sermon was about Peter and John and the lame man who sat in front of the temple every day. The lame man called to the disciples for money but they said, "Silver and gold have we none, but what we have we give to you." Never before had those lines jumped out at me like that. At that point I knew they were offering a lot more than just healing to that lame man.

There were many things I wasn't sure about and I had a lot of questions, but I felt ready to take a leap of faith. I'd take a chance with God and go all the way.

When Smucker gave the altar call, tears were streaming down my face again. But this time I didn't try to hide them. I knew God was calling me and I wasn't going to say no. Other people also went forward that night. It felt so good to pray with each other and share the gladness we felt as God entered our lives and showered us with His love. I didn't receive the baptism of the Holy Spirit that night, but it marked the beginning for me of a closer walk with God. Several people laid hands on me and prayed for me. I also prayed, committing myself fully to God. Then I felt a wonderful release of all my problems and burdens. I felt so happy and had so much love I just had to laugh and cry, it was so good. At that point I never would have believed things could be better, but I found out that the closer you walk with God the more exciting it is. I thought I had experienced everything God had to offer, but this was just the beginning. I had a lot more to learn.

God has so much patience. He knows us so well that He understands how much we can take and when we are ready to face new things. If I had known then all the things that would happen in the next few years, or if I had realized everything God had in store for me, I'm sure I'd have had second thoughts. Also if He had given me any more love or joy, I don't think I could have contained it.

God Gave Me the Gift of Tongues.

After this experience I went to teaching sessions on the Bible whenever I had a chance. They helped me to a closer relationship with Jesus. I had my ups and downs, though, and sometimes became stagnant in my Christian growth. But I was finding out more about the Holy Spirit and His power and love. I was doing a lot of watching, and I observed a difference in people who had been filled with the Holy Spirit.

Sometime later I went to hear a speaker who was a missionary in Honduras. I sensed from the moment he started to speak that Ed King was a man of God and that he was a Spirit-filled Christian. He really had a beautiful way of presenting Jesus.

You're going to think I'm an emotional, cry-easy type of person, but that night I also cried my way through the service. I thought I must be cracking up, or else God was really trying to show me something. After the meeting I went to the speaker and asked him to pray for me to receive the baptism of the Holy Spirit. He and a Spirit-filled lady laid hands on me and prayed very simply.

Nothing happened right away and I thought I didn't really feel any different. But moments later God opened the gates of heaven and let His love stream out and wash over me. I really can't explain how I felt except that if someone had asked me to fly I wouldn't have hesitated. I praised and thanked God over and over again. All of a sudden I wasn't saying words I knew or understood. My mind knew I was praising God and giving all of myself to Him, but I also knew I had never uttered words or sounds like this before. It was a glorious release for me. I found out later that I was speaking in tongues. God had given me a new language to praise Him with.

I know there's controversy about speaking in tongues and many people have a lot of questions about it. I know tongues can be wrongly used. I know that not everyone will speak in tongues who is filled with the Holy Spirit. I know that God loves us and gives us what is best for us.

Please don't misunderstand me as I tell you how it was

with me the first time I spoke in tongues. As I committed my whole being to God, He showered His love and power on me until I felt I couldn't contain it all. The English language was inadequate to express it, so He took my tongue and gave me a new language. Then I found release for some of my deep feelings.

Up to this point I have never used this gift in a meeting where it was interpreted, but for me speaking in tongues is a way to pray. When I don't know how to pray for a certain situation, or I feel such exhilaration and praise for my Father that I cannot express myself in words, then I break into tongues. It's as if God takes away the frustration of not being able to say the things I'm really feeling. My heart knows what I'm saying, but my words are in a strange language.

God took me where I was and started from there. Even with all the power God has, He didn't force me to do things against my will. He took His time and worked things out and brought me into new situations as I was ready. He waited until I was willing to follow.

God uses our Christian brothers and sisters to help us, encourage us, teach us, and lead us back. More and more I see God speaking through people. We really have a responsibility to our Christian brothers and sisters. We are not islands living totally alone.

Fellowship and Praise Help Us to Grow

I've also had to learn that I can't continue to live on that one evening's experiences and that I need to commit myself to Jesus daily. As I take time each day to read God's Word, talk to God, and listen to God, I experience a closer walk with Him. I fail in this so often, though, because I get so busy and caught up with my schoolwork, my friends, and everything else I consider important. Again and again God has to remind me to take time for Him. Surprisingly, when I do I always end up having enough time for everything else too.

Another thing I'm learning is that I need to praise God. I think He really means it when He says, "In everything rejoice, for this is the will of God." It's hard to praise God for those cold chilly mornings when you have to crawl out of bed in an unheated room, or to praise Him for everything that goes wrong in a day. But I'm finding that when I praise God in such situations, and truly mean it, I experience a real peace and feel so much closer to Him. I become more aware of the ways God is working through everything. I believe God has a hand in many more of our "coincidences" than we realize. I know our Father is alive and working in our lives.

I find it hard to sum up the things that I have shared with you and put it all together. What I'm feeling, though, is an excitement for the future—the excitement of walking closer to God and learning to really share everything in a relationship that involves my entire being. I'm excited because I'm a child of the King and He has created me for a reason. He has plans and important things for me to do. Life is not dull anymore.

I know I still have much growing to do and a lot of changes to make and that God has a lot of molding to do with my life. There are many rough edges and humps and bumps to carve and chip away. I want to be open to the Holy Spirit as He leads me on. I am amazed and grateful for God's patience with me and His love for me. He really is a great big wonderful God!

5

FROM PARCHED GROUND TO
LIVING WATERS

Bertha and Paul Swarr

Bertha Shares

During our first several years in Israel, we met a friend
whose life intrigued us as we sensed something of the immediacy and power of God in his life. He was an inde-
pendent missionary. We were challenged to an intangi-
ble reality about his faith, yet something in his overt personality turned us off. He spoke about divine healing and
the baptism of the Spirit, but our minds were closed to
any concepts other than those "secure" ones we had
been taught since childhood.

But this missionary's experiences of the miraculous
ways God provides and his testimonies of God's daily moment-by-moment leading we couldn't forget. Somehow
his "being" communicated more than the words he
shared in conversation. If we had a question or problem,
we intuitively knew Bill would be able to give a word
from the Lord. His ability to feed others from the Bible

Bertha and Paul Swarr have been Mennonite missionaries at Ramat
Gan, Israel, since 1957. Bertha (Wenger) grew up at Versailles,
Missouri; her husband comes from Lancaster, Pennsylvania. Paul
serves as General Secretary of the United Christian Council in Israel,
a fellowship of twenty-one Protestant churches and agencies.

challenged us, though we felt we had quite a good knowledge of the Scriptures ourselves. After all, we had been immersed in them since childhood and studied them in seminary. We could sense, though, that Bill's appetite for the Word of God superseded ours.

The Barrenness of Intellectualism

About ten years of struggle in this seemingly spiritually barren area of the world passed, with all the ups and downs of learning a new language and culture. We shall never despise the firm nurture of childhood and youth, nor the continual sense of the presence of the Lord throughout those years.

In a desperate effort to identify in thought with our local friends in Israel in order to understand them, a good deal of doubt and unbelief crept into my spiritual experience. People here worship the intellect and I had gradually stifled my emotions in preference to an intellectual approach to faith. I began to forget that there is no real conflict between an intellectual approach to faith and the emotion of a love response to God. I also neglected a daily feeding on the Word, partly out of busyness, but also from a lack of appetite, receiving from the Bible only the deductions of my mind. Prayer became a perfunctory habit and sense of responsibility. I knew it was important and did not really want to go backward spiritually, but I was frustrated and discouraged.

We were not alone in our frustration. Several couples with similar experiences banded together to share deeply on a heart-to-heart level in prayer and discussion.

About this time another couple came to join us—a

staid Britisher, born Anglican, who worked as BOAC air-port manager, and his wife. We loved Dorothy and Aubrey, and sensed something contagious about their vital contact with God. We learned that they both had had a Pentecostal experience, which seemed to have changed the formality of their faith into something living and real. Somehow they had an inner knowledge and power about them which we wanted, and yet this didn't make them "strange" people, unpredictable and noisy as we had the impression Pentecostal people were. They wisely and carefully kept placing before us the possibility of the something more in our relationship with God which the baptism in the Holy Spirit brings. Their lives of love and effectiveness underscored the truth of their words.

From them, and from other sources, came to us books such as John Sherrill's *They Speak with Other Tongues,* Agnes Sanford's *The Healing Gifts of the Spirit,* and Robert Frost's, *Aglow with the Spirit.* Our hearts were stirred as we glimpsed possibilities we had not seen before.

Somehow we had concluded that miracles were for New Testament times, but not for today, and that the spiritual gifts spoken of in the New Testament were natural talents and nothing more.

At this point we had reached an all-time low in dis-couragement and decided either that God must break forth in our lives and witness in a new way, or we were giving up—at least here in Israel!

We were discouraged—but also fearful. We didn't want to leave the safe moorings of the interpretations we had been reared with, and surely didn't want to become emotional fanatics. Our friends' lives proved to us, however, that that wasn't necessary.

The Gentle Spirit Won Our Hearts

Then the truth became clear to us through our longtime friend whom we had "tuned out" for so many years: "Never doubt the presence of the Spirit in your life if you are a believer. You can't even believe without Him. But always keep open for an increased understanding of Him and yieldedness to Him. The baptism of the Spirit is not for salvation, but bestows power for service."

With this realization the fears vanished and suddenly new vistas appeared—new possibilities—new aware-nesses of the reality of God.

In a small gathering of our prayer partners, I asked that hands be placed upon me that I might receive from God a newness of Himself which I desperately wanted and glimpsed and yet could not fully comprehend. I simply wanted more of God!

My pride was broken. I admitted that I had a need and I told God that I'd even be willing to talk in tongues if that's what it took.

As prayer was made for me, I sensed an inner release which expressed itself in a deep weeping. An inner prayer formed itself in the words, "Lord, I believe. Help thou my unbelief." I have come to understand that this emotion was given by the Spirit, for it unlocked the door to my spiritual dryness, sterility, and frustration.

From this time on things began to happen. A new faith awakened within me. I was hungry for the Word. Each time I opened the Bible, truths leapt forth which I had not seen before. All I had read about the life in the Spirit (in which I had previously thought I was fully walking) now became clear. I now loved to pray and just wanted to worship God for who He is! I began to discover an inner sense of direction—"Do this; don't do that." A new love for people, including my husband and children, caused life to glow with meaning. I became aware of ways in which my personality and life needed changing to match the inner promptings I was receiving as I read and thought about the person of Jesus.

I still wanted to talk in tongues because I felt that somehow I didn't quite "have it all," but I just couldn't. I tried making strange sounds like the books said, but it didn't make any sense to me. Actually, I was seeking an experience rather than God, the Giver. I was craving the emotional sensation I expected to receive.

I was a bit discouraged. I had expected that some ecstasy would come upon me from outside and make my tongue start speaking. Then it became clear to me that a prayer language will not be understood by my mind. It is not an ecstatic experience, but rather the accepting by cool faith a gift which God offers, and that I should begin speaking with the faith, that what I willingly began, God would fill with His content. (We hear many languages here in Israel and when someone prays in a language I don't understand it surely doesn't disturb me. Why, therefore, should I be distressed over a heavenly prayer language which my mind cannot understand?)

And so I thanked God for His gift which I had not yet used, but which I told Him I wanted to receive. Concentrating on thoughts of praise and thanks, I began to make sounds. Gradually I became aware that these sounds began to make a pattern of sentences. They issued from my very soul and brought an inner release and often a clear understanding of what they meant. I felt like a little child learning to walk and then to run. I am now most grateful for this gift, not only for praising God, but also for giving expression to those inner promptings too deep for words, but which long for expression.

God would never have imposed this gift upon me against my will, for He *offers* rather than *forces* us to receive His gifts. But how much I would be missing had I remained too proud or unaware to accept and use this gift! God's gifts are too precious and blessed to be despised or refused!

Learners in the School of the Spirit

There are times of doubt because I wanted to feel I had arrived at a certain spiritual level. But I began to realize that I was just opening the door a crack into a previously unknown world of wonder, joy, and challenge! There was so much I didn't know, whereas before I felt I had been quite well acquainted with God. I hadn't realized then that one can never grasp all there is to know of the love, the wonder, and the glory of God and the sheer joy of the gift of salvation.

Life in this new dimension has its moments of ecstasy, but it is mostly a cool, calm, walk of faith in moment-by-moment obedience to the inner promptings of the Spirit, constantly checked and in agreement with the written Word, and in subjection and conjunction with fellow members in the body of Christ, and through whomever God chooses to speak.

The school of the Spirit has included lessons in the

miraculous, of actually hearing the voice of God, and other very real and deep experiences. These have been the by-products of worship, rather than experiences sought after in themselves.

The Lord has moved in a new way, in response to my quickened faith, in our family and circle of friends. There have been miracles of healing, some instantaneous and some more gradual. Some of these healings have been in the physical realm, but others have been healings of memories, resentments, and situations requiring repentance and forgiveness.

I could recount almost endlessly the vivid evidences of the reality of the Lord's presence and leading in my life. This new life in the Spirit has helped me minister to others whose depths of need I would and could not have attempted to meet without the power, wisdom, and knowledge which the Spirit gives. At the same time, I experience immeasurable joy in an inner ministry of praise to God, an ever growing love for Him, and an increasing awareness of the vistas of power and possibility in God yet to be learned and put into practice. All praise to Him!

Paul Shares

On a Sabbath afternoon in 1970 twelve persons had gathered in a living room at the Baptist Village in Israel. We were discussing the implications of Agnes Sanford's book, *The Healing Gifts of the Spirit*. Someone dared to say, "If we truly believe that God's power is as available today as it was to Peter and John, why don't we pray right now for the healing of Mrs. Smith's back?" We all knew that her back had been stiff and calcified following a fall six years before. And for all her British determination, Mrs. Smith already had seventy years to her credit, an age when bones tend to be brittle and backs are inclined not to bend.

Nevertheless, we circled around Mary Smith to pray. Prayer always seems a proper thing to do. I joined with the others in serious intention. But I did not expect anything unusual to happen. I had never been taught to *ask* God for a miracle. My theology urged me to *wait* rather fatalistically for whatever He graciously might grant.

Her sudden outcry, "I'm healed, I'm healed!" startled me. Amazed, I opened my eyes. "Help me to my feet, brethren," she demanded. In less than a minute the lady with the stiff back was touching the floor with the palms of her hands! (At 40, I didn't care to duplicate her calisthenics.) My mind was boggled, my thoughts were jammed. I had just witnessed a First Century miracle! Then spontaneously we all prayed and praised and rejoiced and shouted, "Blessed be the Lord God of Israel who only does wondrous things. Hallelujah!"

That was the key that opened the door for me into a whole new realm of faith. Now I knew that God is able miraculously and instantaneously to pour His healing power into a human body even in the Twentieth Century. "This miracle was not merely for the sake of my old body," Mrs. Smith told us, "but so that the body of Christ here in Tel Aviv will grow in faith." And that was what began to happen.

Sketches of Divine Leading

No two people experience God's salvation in identical

ways, even if those persons happen to be husband and wife. Growing in the Spirit is like that, too. Experiences are as varied as the many indistinguishable hues of a perfect rainbow. Bertha and I were together in our spiritual search. The circumstances were like parallel paths for us. Yet each of us needed to taste God's goodness for ourselves.

I vividly recall the thirst for God that took me to college. I wanted an education for life ahead, but desperately needed a loving Father to show me how best to use the training. The tiny upper room on the top floor of the Administration Building taught me as much as many a lecture. There, as young men, my buddies and I met God, and there we became brothers. It was a flaming bush, a training ground of the Spirit.

When Bertha and I were married at a rural church in Missouri, we chose to sing a prayer-testimony: "Lord, possess us now, we pray. . . . With Thy Spirit, fill us." Like Peter with Jesus on the Mount of Transfiguration, we didn't know all we were saying. And yet God graciously answered that prayer in His own time and way. It's been an exciting pilgrimage.

Ontario, Connecticut, Pennsylvania, and Colorado— as with many young couples, we had no continuing city. Then Israel—land of the modern pioneer, of irrigated deserts, of cities built on sand dunes and drained malarial swamps. This was an exhilarating new life, the homeland for our three children.

But we soon discovered that a modern metropolis with a secular spirit can be a desert for the soul. We floundered. Oh, I still loved God, but I had lost much of the reality of His touch on my life. I had absorbed more of

the spirit of this strange land than I had of His offered
Spirit.

In the mid-Sixties one of our Baptist colleagues called
together about five couples to form a prayer cell. We all
had insurmountable problems and pains in our plans and
projects. We didn't know what to do. So we prayed. And
that was the beginning of a discovery. For God not only
changed some of our projects, He also changed us.

In looking back, I marvel at the ways of God. He knew
our desperation. He had sent us leanness of soul so that
we would seek His face. Now He sent us books. He sent
us cassettes. He sent us men. Men like Michael Harper
and Ralph Mahoney, Costa Deir and Bahjat Batarseh,
and others such as Corrie ten Boom and David Pawson.
And many lesser-known persons gave of their love to us.
There was the young Anglican couple from Auckland,
New Zealand, who, like Aquila and Priscilla, expounded
to us the way of God more accurately. There was the
retired Mennonite bishop from Argentina who spent a
refreshing weekend with our team. There was the Me-
thodist minister from Kentucky who lived in our home
for three months. Could I not learn the value of a three-
day fast from a man who had learned the values of a
forty-day fast? Our whole family was touched. "Uncle
Richard" affected our eating habits as well as our prayer
life.

We soon discovered that these persons were not
perfect. They too were on a pilgrimage with feet of clay.
But they all testified of dimensions of life in the Spirit
which were beyond our present experience. In turn, we
began to realize more and more the value of hungering
and thirsting after righteousness.

Miracles of Healing

The group that experienced the miracle of Mrs. Smith's healed back became a living prayer-link of faith. Emergency needs were telephoned from person to person. Faith leaped to expect God to act. A TWA pilot's wife, previously unknown to any of us, was deathly sick with peritonitis. She was anointed with oil in her hospital bed by the Anglican priest, while the community of believers offered prayers of faith in their own homes. Her quick recovery astonished all who were not aware of the secret. A Jewish lad, seriously injured in a motorcycle collision, was prayed for by believers while he lingered two weeks in a coma. A sister in Christ felt moved to go to his hospital bed and pray in the Spirit for him while he lay unconscious. The next day he was off the critical list.

Then one morning Bertha came to the breakfast table without her glasses. She had worn glasses for twenty years, since her early teens. "I think God wants to teach me a special lesson," she told me. I was thrown off balance. Almost everyone wears glasses, I thought. We really don't want our friends to think we're becoming eccentric or fanatic. There must be limits, even to a good thing.

But in the days that followed it became clear that Bertha was believing God for the healing of her eyes. She seemed intuitively to sense that this was something very personal between her and the Lord, a delicate lesson in total obedience precisely in a realm where the mind says no. "I promised the Lord," Bertha declared, "that when people ask me what happened to my eyes, whether believers or the shopkeepers across the street, I will testify that God did this for me to show that Jesus is alive today!"

How carefully we must tread became evident when our young daughter descended the stairs another morning announcing, "If Jesus can heal Mommie's eyes, He surely is able to heal mine, too." She had worn glasses since four years of age. Somehow God restrained us from spoiling her tender faith. I had thought we could make adult decisions that would only affect ourselves, but wasn't prepared for this turn in the road. Now, six years later, mother and daughter both have 20/20 vision, according to the oculist. All glory to God! It was more than a momentary touch.

And though Mrs. Smith has other infirmities of old age, her back is still healed. Meanwhile, I am still wearing glasses. I accept this as part of the mystery and beauty of God's dealing differently with differing people.

Slain in the Spirit

However, the Lord has continued to nudge me on in responsiveness to Him. One Wednesday evening a prayer cell of seven persons met in a little cottage by the Jaffa seashore. By "chance," I had traveled that day from Caesarea to Jaffa (ancient Joppa), as the friends of Cornelius had done. That night God revealed Himself to me in a way that was as real as Peter's vision on a Jaffa housetop. As we prayed and worshiped, the bright light of God's presence permeated that living room. Oblivious of the others, I was knocked to the floor. The cottage became a Holy of Holies, a meeting place with the living God in whose presence I could not stand up. I was drained of all strength.

Then I knew that Isaiah 6 and Acts 9 were flesh-and-blood experiences. As we left that home, I imagined that

I understood how Lazarus must have felt as he was unraveled from his graveclothes and set free again to live! Yet, rightly or wrongly, I have told few persons about this experience until now. There are meetings with God, a bathing of the inner being, which are too personal and sacred to share lest they become stale and defiled in the telling. And yet how dull the Scriptures would be if they contained only theology, without the illustrative experiences of Abraham and David, of Jeremiah and Peter. Therefore, I write.

The Jaffa experience unlocked more doors. There was a freshness about the Scriptures which I had lost. Truth leaped from the page. Prayer became a greater joy, praise and worship a natural privilege. Scripture verses set to music punctuated our homelife. It was even easier to get up in the morning! In essence, I think the change centered around the fact that I was allowing Jesus a fresh centrality in my thoughts and activities. I could never love Him enough, but I was learning to love Him more and more. His blood-covering for my sin became more precious. The power and authority of Jesus' name took on a new meaning.

Drinking Deeply of New Experiences

With the freshness of love for Jesus came another discovery. I could now see more of Jesus in other people. It was easier to forgive and to experience forgiveness. Denominational walls have crumbled as the floodtide of the Spirit has risen. Fellow ministers and missionaries have become colleagues, rather than competitors, in kingdom work. We have sensed that together we are to be elders over the flock of God in this city. This broadening has also included Roman Catholic brethren. God loves all His children and is at work renewing us all.

A practical change happened in our home. God seemed to be teaching us that the walls of our house were to be expanded to include more than the five members of our natural family. We've had our growing pains over this one. But in the past six years quite a few brothers and sisters have spent some months, few or many, at our table. These have included a Nigerian student and an Australian dental nurse, a retarded teenager and an Israeli soldier girl, a British piano teacher and several American students. Beauty shone through when our own teenagers urged us as parents to welcome yet others into the family. We have been more blessed than burdened.

Another lesson the Lord taught me was that I should not seek any of His gifts, however good, for its own sake. It happened this way. For some time I had observed the anointing of God on the lives of various friends who I knew spent much time praying in the Spirit. Therefore, I desired this gift of a prayer language. I agonized with the Lord about this longing of mine for more than a year. Meanwhile, our children seemingly had so easily received this blessing at first request. Thank God, children aren't as complicated in their faith relationship to a loving Father as we adults are.

One Friday afternoon, three of us had gathered in our living room for special prayer for a musician friend. He was the conductor of the Singers of Praise Choir, and we were to give a concert that same evening. Ilana, his wife, had telephoned to report that he had developed a deep bronchial-type congestion in his chest and would not be able to conduct that evening. We had no assistant conductor. As we three lifted this need into the Lord's presence, I felt strangely compelled to stretch out my hands as if to place them upon my sick brother who was in his own bed ten miles away. My arms felt electrified with the Lord's power. Then, almost unnoticed at first, as I interceded for my brother a prayer language softly flowed from my lips. I had not been thinking about praying in tongues at that moment. God had graciously granted my heart's desire when my attention centered on the needs of my brother, and not upon the gift itself. It was an important lesson.

That evening our musician brother conducted the concert. God had restored him for the task. And a new gift from the Lord rested in a very earthen vessel, as I learned to pray in the Spirit, allowing syllables of worship which bypassed my mind to ascend like incense into the presence of His throne room. How precious this gift has become as many times the desires of my heart, which are beyond words, have needed to be voiced by His Spirit in me to the Father. What a joy to praise Him with my whole being. All of God's gifts are good gifts and to be desired of Him. All praise to Jesus!

Growing Toward Maturity

What are some of the other lessons He seems to be teaching us? We have learned to turn first to God for healing, rather than as a last resort when medicine fails. We still respect and appreciate the medical profession and all those God calls into this ministry.

We have learned that terminology regarding any experience is not as important as the reality of falling at His feet. We are learning to see the need and value of both the fruit of the Spirit and the gifts of the Spirit in the lives of individual believers and in the gathered assembly. We have tried to avoid icy orthodoxy as much as frothy fanaticism in the longing to see both Word and Spirit incarnated in our lives.

We are learning not to impose our own experiences as a necessary pattern for others, but only to testify of the goodness of God in our lives. We have needed all we have received. We have been greatly blessed, yet we desire still more of His fullness. We recognize that no one spiritual experience is a cure-all for the latent wayward-ness of our hearts. We have not become super-Christians. But we are glad and grateful to have moved a notch from our earlier spiritual dryness and desperation.

We are deeply concerned when we hear some say that renewal in the Holy Spirit is dangerous and divisive. Our experience has been the opposite. The Spirit has drawn us together in a greater unity than we knew before, for this is the work of the Spirit. Of course, even salvation is a divisive experience, dividing the responsive from the unresponsive, causing those who remain on the sidelines to be a bit suspicious of what is happening inside the circle. Nonetheless, it is incumbent upon all who are on the "inside" of any experience to interpret it in such a way that it will bless and benefit others, not hurt nor needlessly divide.

All of life is not made up of unusual experiences. There's a lot of everyday plodding. But our feet are lighter now. We have not gone far on the journey with Jesus. But we are certain He has much more to teach us.

Blessed be the Trinity: Father, Son, and Spirit!

6

A PREACHER'S KID WHO MADE IT

Allen J. Yoder

Much Theory, Little Experience

Persons often claim great things for the Christian life—victory, joy, peace, power, love, brotherhood, and the like—all apparently scriptural and yet, for most of us, they seem just out of reach. Some of us change the script and say it's not for our day. Others claim they have arrived even though their experience doesn't bear them out. Some say, "Only believe, you don't need an emotional experience." Some just give up.

For myself, life has been a constant search—a pressing forward. I have chosen to believe that what God says in His Word can be mine in reality—not only as a spiritual realization, but as a practical reality in my life. So when the Bible says, "The old has passed away, behold, the new has come" (2 Corinthians 5:17), I believe this should be a reality in my experience. I'm not interested in mental gymnastics. If what I hear in the sermon on Sunday doesn't work in my life on Monday, then forget it.

Allen and Anita Yoder live at Siletz, Oregon, where he is dean of students at the Siletz Public School. Earlier he was vice-principal at Western Mennonite School, Salem, Oregon, and taught there for nine years. He received his master's degree from the University of Oregon.

At a point in my life several years ago, I felt myself becoming cynical. I had accepted Christ at a tender age, grew up as a Mennonite minister's kid, went to Mennonite schools, married a Mennonite girl, and finally came back to teach in a Mennonite school.

I was a "good" boy as I was growing up. I never smoked nor drank nor did many of the "bad" things. I really tried to live the Christian life. Yet throughout those years, and even after I was teaching in a Christian school, Satan still had me in bondage in whole areas of my life.

I did enjoy many experiences of growth and enlarged understanding in my Christian pilgrimage. I knew I belonged to the Lord, and yet I was not really aware of many of the implications of this—both in the areas of privileges and responsibilities.

Introduction to Reality

After graduation from college in 1965, I took a job teaching in a public school near Seattle, Washington. Since there was no Mennonite congregation there, we worshiped with a small community church. I felt this would be a good time to sort out the "cultural" from the "scriptural" in my experience, so I decided to search the Word for myself as never before. It was here that I experienced one of the first real milestones in my Christian life.

Prior to this I wanted to study the Word, yet it wasn't really all that exciting to me. Often I wound up going to sleep before many verses had been digested. Finally, in exasperation, I told the Lord, "If You want me to get anything out of Bible study, You'll have to make it a lot more interesting." I prayed, "Lord, open the Word to me in an exciting new way." God answered that prayer immediately. All of a sudden the New Testament became alive. When I picked it up to read it, I could read a whole book or two in one sitting. "What's happening?" I asked myself several days later. Bible study was becoming a beautiful experience.

One of the things that came alive to me during that year was the earthshaking conviction, "Jesus lives in me! 'It is no longer I who live, but Christ who lives in me; and the life I now live in the flesh I live by faith in the Son of God, who loved me and gave himself for me' " (Galatians 2:20). I had said it many times myself and had heard it in countless sermons, "Jesus lives in my heart," but it had never struck home before. The very Creator of the universe is alive in me! Incredible! I began to draw more and more from His strength and to rely less and less on mine.

The following year I accepted a teaching position at Western Mennonite School near Salem, Oregon. It proved to be a year of testing. In the busyness of my schedule I often didn't spend time in the Word. My life reached another plateau. I felt that I was in the place where God wanted me, and I attempted to minister there, but I became more and more dissatisfied. In spite of my close relationship with Christ and the opportunity of teaching in a Christian setting, many areas of my life were still totally un-Christlike.

Desperation Point

A year or so after going to Western, I entered summer school at the University of Oregon to work on a master's degree. It was there that some of my problems began to surface. I was faced with many temptations. I was too conscientious to give in and sin openly, yet I knew that for me all things were not new. I still had a lot of the "old man" kicking around in me. The intensity of my struggle multiplied. There seemed to be no answers.

But I saw things happening to a number of my friends and acquaintances that awakened new hope in me. People who had been mediocre Christians were suddenly becoming alive, victorious, joyful, witnessing Christians. In the desperation of my hunger, I was drawn to them. I didn't ask many outright questions, but I continued to observe them closely. Eventually I found out that they had been "filled with the Spirit," or had received the "baptism in the Holy Spirit," as some called it. I began to look into this experience for myself.

During my third summer at the university I finally came to the end of myself. All my life I had struggled with certain temptations and sins. I decided to struggle no more. "Jesus," I prayed, "You will need to change my desires, and create a new heart in me. If You can't do it, I'm through with Christianity."

Like a bolt of lightning God showed me I had been sinning in attempting to overcome Satan in my own strength, rather than simply accepting by faith the victory that Christ had already won on Calvary.

At this point, I believe I was as emptied of self as I had ever been before in my life. But still I struggled. Finally, I came to God with an ultimatum. "Either You change me, or I'll just go ahead and do the things I desire to do. I refuse to struggle anymore." I was dead serious. I would literally have given my right arm, even my life at that point, to know the total reality of victory in Jesus. I prayed, "God, fill me with Your Holy Spirit." My cards were all on the table. It was all or nothing in the Christian life for me now.

Reality Breaks Through

In the days that followed, I was almost afraid to leave my room, for I had vowed not to fight Satan in my own strength anymore. What if it didn't work? What if all those old desires were still there? I went out literally trembling. With each step I whispered a prayer, "It's all up to You Lord. You'll have to do it, Holy Spirit. I can't."

I'm not sure how many days it took me to realize it, but my desires were changed! Praise God! I was a new creature in Him. Old things had passed away! Behold, all things had become new! The struggles and guilt which had dogged me since early childhood were gone! Each time I whispered that prayer, "It's up to You, Holy Spirit," He came through. Life became more beautiful each day. I had a song in my heart and I was free! Hallelujah!

One of the most wonderful things God did for me was to give me an insatiable craving for the Word. Sometimes before it was interesting and even exciting whenever I took time to read it, but now I couldn't put it down. For a whole year I seldom went to bed before 2:00 or 3:00 A.M. My hunger for the Word was so great that I literally had to force myself to lay it down and get a few hours of sleep.

Now whole new areas of the Bible became alive to me. I began to study more about the Holy Spirit and His work. I read few books and talked to few people about it.

It seemed God limited me up to Himself and His Word
for that year. A fire burned in my bones. I couldn't get
enough of God or the Bible.

As time went on, I began to encounter other people
who had similar experiences. I saw tremendous changes
in their lives also.

I began to attend Full Gospel Business Men's meetings
and was tremendously touched and enriched by the love
and worship I experienced there. Fellowship in the
Spirit, with that free flow of praise, became something I
thirsted for. Almost desperately I went from one meeting
to another because I did not find that same fellowship in
many of my Mennonite circles.

It was a time of beautiful growth and discovery.
However, it seemed that one fellow had my number. No
matter where I went to a meeting, he showed up—
whether it was in Eugene, Salem, or Portland. Each time
he met me he insisted, "If you haven't spoken in
tongues, you haven't received the baptism with the Holy
Spirit." Then he'd slap me on the back and inquire,
"Have you got it yet?" I never knew what to say. He
really bugged me. I began to wonder if I really was filled
with the Spirit. I went forward at a Full Gospel Meeting
to make sure, but I couldn't bring myself to follow their
instructions and begin to "jabber," as it seemed to me
then. Finally a Spirit-filled, tongue-speaking, Baptist
minister friend of mine said to me, "Al, I believe you've
already been filled with the Spirit. Just thank Him and
quit asking." It was good advice. Accepting the fullness
of the Spirit is a step of faith just as with salvation—we
simply ask and receive by faith.

How I praised the Lord that this problem was finally

settled! I still felt from my study of the Scripture, however, that a prayer language of praise and worship was available to every Spirit-filled believer, but I didn't have it. I talked with my Dad about it. He said, "Son, tongues are not the essential thing. Simply seek the Giver of the gift and learn to praise and worship Him."

The following summer I was back at the University of Oregon and anxious to witness for the Lord. However, the Lord arranged a clerical error so that I lived in a double room with no roommate. This was the opportunity I needed to practice praise.

At first five minutes seemed forever. What was there to say? "Praise the Lord! Uh, good night, Lord!" I simply didn't know how to praise and worship Him for more than a few minutes. However, as time went on I began to spend more time in praise, using the psalms and different choruses I had learned. Soon I was spending half an hour, then an hour each night in praise and worship. One of those nights as I was praising the Lord, I couldn't find adequate words to express myself. Suddenly, I knew that I could pray in the Spirit. Just that simply I began to pray in an unknown tongue. I continued praising Him in my new prayer tongue for half an hour, lost in my love for Him. Since that time, whenever I'm praising, if I choose to do so, I can pray in tongues and through the Holy Spirit offer acceptable praise and worship. This blessed privilege came almost exactly a year after I was filled with the Spirit.

Anita's Struggle with Me

I have mentioned little about my wife and my story would not be complete without including her. During the time when I was desperately searching, and when I began to find such sweet fellowship at meetings with other Spirit-filled Christians, I left my wife sitting at home with the children. Deep resentment began to build up in her. While she didn't oppose my doctrine, neither could she accept it because it took me away from her at times when she needed me very much. I also resented her, because she was trying to squelch the very thing which brought such joy to me. She did admit that in many ways I became a better father and husband, yet she couldn't quite forgive me for leaving her so much.

It has taken us a number of years to restore some of the damage done to our marriage through my blindness and lack of patience. Because of my shortsightedness, it was a long time before my wife was able to claim the fullness of the Spirit freely in her own life.

Anita had prayed for the fullness of the Spirit often, but couldn't seem to find the freedom in praise that I was experiencing. Finally one night she shared her problem with me. "Each time I try to raise my hands in praise, I see you leaving me to go to another meeting. I have not been able to forgive you." That night we both asked forgiveness of each other, and the Lord initiated a healing process that is still continuing. Praise God He's in the healing business.

There has been so much more. The baptism in the Holy Spirit is not the end—it is only the door that leads to a beautiful walk in the Spirit. I enjoyed sharing in planning the Rejoice 75 Holy Spirit celebration conference at Western Mennonite School. I have also visited other groups where the Lord is pouring out His Spirit. I praise God that the Mennonite Church is returning to more openness to the work of the Spirit and some of the applications which our Anabaptist forefathers understood and practiced much better than we.

Anita and I are now involved in a sharing community, for we believe that the gifts of the Spirit only become operative and meaningful in the context of a caring, close-knit body of believers.

We have visited Reba Place Fellowship in Evanston, Illinois, and the Church of the Redeemer in Houston, Texas. We believe that these, as well as the Book of Acts, are examples of the Spirit at work in the body. We are exploring further what this kind of lifestyle can really mean to the church. Pray for us.

7

A DOCTOR WHO FOUND THE DEEPER HEALING

Harry L. Kraus, MD

Tragedy and No Resources to Meet It

In the summer of 1957, one year after setting up medical practice in rural Newport News, I stopped at my office on the way home from the hospital. The telephone was ringing as I unlocked the door. When I answered, the voice was a friend who lived along the river, telling me that my boys were in an accident on the sandbar and that I should hurry down.

"How bad an accident?" I asked with my heart seeming to stand still.

"Pretty bad," she answered. "You'd better come right away."

When I got there no boys were in sight. There was nothing but a narrow beach and water. The flood tide covered the bar completely. At ages seven and nine they had just learned to swim a few strokes. Full of confidence, they had ventured too far out and were pulled into the deep water by the strong tide.

Harry and Mildred (Brunk) Kraus live at Newport News, Virginia, where Harry is a family physician. He was born at Hyattsville, Maryland, and received his medical training from the Medical College of Virginia.

Mildred and I struggled to put our lives back together after this terrible tragedy. How did God expect us to react? I tried to make full confession of my youthful sins to Mildred, but was not fully able to come clean. I had heard of God becoming more real to people through a crisis experience. For a short time I honestly tried to establish a closer relationship to Him, but without much success. Soon I was back in my old ways, making my own rules to fit my situation.

Mildred and I, with our only children taken from us, felt suddenly alone. We found that we had little communication going between us anymore. The burden became unbearable for her and only the grace of God saved her life in a serious suicide attempt.

Plenty of Form but Little Power

"Having a form of godliness, but denying the power thereof"—these words from 2 Timothy 3:5 were familiar to me as a Mennonite lay worker and teacher. I was quick to apply them to the modernist who denied the atonement through the blood of Christ, or to some other group who questioned the Virgin birth, but never to myself, for I was a good Mennonite, and my parents were Mennonites.

But somehow, somewhere down deep inside me, I became increasingly aware that my godliness was more form than fact and that I was experiencing little power in life. I didn't connect this with verses 2-7 of 2 Timothy 3 even though behind my form of godliness facade many of these sins of the spirit and flesh were true of me from time to time. As I look back I think I knew the power of God unto salvation of Romans 1:16, but very little of the power for victorious living of Romans 8, or the power of witnessing of Acts 1:8.

I grew up in a sheltered Mennonite community with all my friends coming from the same church setting. Of course we went to school with "others," but we were careful to keep those relationships quite casual. I was sure that my church which taught the "whole Bible," including nonconformity to the world and nonresistance, was superior to all others. My witness to this superiority was my willingness to wear the nonconformed garb, and later my conscientious objector stand in World War II.

In all fairness, I think my parents and the church leaders had a more mature concept of Christianity than I did. The Sunday sermons and my home teaching made plain the basic facts of the plan of salvation, so that as a child I understood what was required and confessed Jesus Christ as my Savior. In fact I cannot recall a time when I did not know the basic outline of the Bible.

Outward and Inner Uncertainty

It was my privilege to attend Eastern Mennonite School at Harrisonburg, Virginia, for my senior year of high school. There I learned to know Mildred Brunk, who four years later became my wife. Those were war years. In 1944 my deferment was canceled and I received my "greetings from the president." As a conscientious objector from one of the historic peace churches I served two years in Civilian Public Service (CPS) camps.

The idea of becoming a physician was born while working in a CPS unit at a mental hospital. When I was released from my service assignment in 1946 I was impatient to get married and start living, so I accepted a job working my uncle's orchard. Mildred and I were married in October 1946. A year later our family expanded with the birth of a son. It was becoming clear to me that I would never be satisfied working in an orchard, so when the opportunity came to enter Eastern Mennonite College we moved to Harrisonburg.

In 1950 our second son was born. The following year I graduated from college and we moved to Richmond to attend the Medical College of Virginia. I trusted God to help me through medical school. I worked summers and nights and borrowed money anywhere I could to pay my way through medical training. On the outside I still maintained my form of godliness but on the inside I was spiritually almost bankrupt.

It is difficult to write openly of one's inner duplicity. It seems so depressing and stupid, and yet how else can one bear witness to what God has done? While maintaining the outer "sheep's clothing" (church attendance, committee work, Sunday school teaching, tithing, and the like) there remained the sneak use of tobacco, the occasional hidden pornography, and the wolf's immorality.

Along with these, I harbored theological doubts about the literal existence of hell. The Bible became a book which "contained the Word of God" instead of "being the Word of God."

One of the ways in which I worked hard at maintaining my cover was studying the Bible. I really desired to be the person God wanted me to be, but found myself defeated again and again. I don't regret at all those hours spent in study. They seemed significant then, but as I look back there really weren't that many of them. However, God's Word is powerful and does not return to

Him void, and I'm sure that what good there was in my life was a result of His faithful Word in me.

A Wearisome Routine of Ups and Downs

Married life was a mixture of blessings and failures. In May 1959, nearly two years after the drownings, Mildred presented us with twin girls. In September 1960 another boy arrived, born on my birthday. These children were miracles. Mildred had suffered four miscarriages after our second son's birth, and we had given up hope of having more children. Truly God's mercy and goodness are beyond our comprehension.

Mildred went through a series of depressions, partly because she knew that something was wrong inside me, but she could never really put her finger on it. We thank God for psychiatrists, sleeping pills, tranquilizers, and antidepressants. But these were not cures. They only helped to make life bearable.

It is possible to fall into an attitude toward life that totally precludes victorious living and leads one into situational ethics. The rationale goes something like this: Christianity was introduced into the world with a spectacular display of power, insights, healings, angel appearances, deliverances, prophecies, tongues, and other supernatural manifestations. This type of power, however, faded out with the death of the twelve apostles. Since that time these promises, having already been fulfilled, are no longer applicable to us. Having been born into the kingdom of God, one now relies on the printed Word of God.

This is the feeble situation many of us are in. We try to make the best of it and work out our own salvation with fear and trembling. With part of the salvation story no longer accepted as true, it is easy to ignore other teachings. For example, business entanglements with unbelievers are okay. Confession of faults one to another would create too disruptive a situation in the church, so this is played down. Praising the Lord creates a disturbance, so we tend to keep quiet.

In my case, I argued within myself that confessing my sins to Mildred would endanger her life with further depression and so was situationally unwise. Certainly this was not what God would want. I didn't believe that God would honor His Word to "make all things abound toward us" including a healing of her depressions. Year after year I continued on the same plateau, wanting to live for God but lacking the power for a happy, victorious life.

Many times during these years, Mildred and I answered the call to rededicate ourselves to the Lord. We went forward at meetings, expressing our desire to be right with Him. We even went forward to receive the Holy Spirit in a tent meeting in the 1950s, but it turned out to be no more than a call to rededication. I found no power to live in the Spirit through these experiences.

Finally a Breakthrough

Our breakthrough began with Mildred. Awakened to the existence of a better life, she began reading—sporadically at first, but then with slowly accelerating pace. In 1972 she persuaded me to attend a Basic Youth Conflicts Seminar. This had to be of the Lord for my ego told me I was not a youth, I knew the Bible, as a physician I certainly was aware of youth conflicts, and why should I

go listen to some hotshot youth director? But it was a
chance for a vacation and I knew we needed to be
together, so we went. It was there that I was made to face
the fact that the Bible is really true, that we can't adjust
it to fit our situations, and that God always honors His
Word.

At a Dave Wilkerson Crusade a physician colleague
from Newport News, Paul Givens and his wife, Barbara,
came up to us after a meeting beaming and praising the
Lord. This just wasn't in character for them. We listened
with surprise and a little shock as they told us en-
thusiastically that they had experienced the baptism of
the Spirit. They had received the Holy Spirit while
listening to the 700 Club on the Christian Broadcasting
Network. Of course we said that was wonderful.

But on the way home I turned to Mildred and asked,
"Just what did they mean—baptized with the Spirit?"
We didn't get too excited because we knew that the
"Second Work of Grace" was a heresy that had been
around for a long time and had created a lot of havoc in
various churches.

About the same time the Lord sent a young man to
enter the family practice residency program at Riverside
Hospital. Dave was turned on to the Lord and soon had a
Christian Medical Society group started. We participated
and watched with envy as one of the doctors accepted the
Lord, then whizzed on past us in his Christian life, in his
zeal for spiritual things, and in his vigorous study of the
Bible. He had sought and found the baptism of the Holy
Ghost, and what a difference it made in him.

For the first time in our lives we were a part of a small
fellowship of persons who had similar interests and were

unashamedly seeking God's will and way in their lives. We read a number of books on the Holy Spirit and became convinced that we had been ignorant of God's marvelous provision for victorious living. About this time, too, we became aware of the experience of Dan and Martha Yutzy, which helped us accept the idea of Spirit baptism as a valid experience. We even allowed one couple to pray with us for the baptism, but nothing happened.

I felt like I knew what was keeping this blessing of God from us. I still was not being completely honest with Mildred about my past. She had not needed tranquilizers or antidepressants after the Basic Youth Conflicts Seminar, but was still on sleeping pills. I discussed with the psychiatrist my making full confession to her but he warned against it, saying that she wouldn't be able to live with it. I couldn't get free of the feeling, however, that God really meant whatever He said, and I promised Him that I would be obedient to what He told me to do in His own timing.

In July 1974 our children were away for a weekend and Mildred and I were alone at home. We had a lovely Saturday together. On Sunday morning I awoke early with the distinct feeling that God was saying "Harry, now's the time." I protested and continued to say, "But God, You know what it will do to her," and He just repeated, "Now's the time." I said, "God, You'll have to show me better than that." Well, He just melted me with weeping. Mildred awoke and began to comfort me and ask me to tell her everything, and I did. There was joy, forgiveness, peace, and love as Mildred was able to pass the burden right over to the Lord as it all spilled out. We never enjoyed such a glorious time together before as the next fifteen hours.

Prayer Languages for Two Grateful People

Then followed 2½ days of terrific attack. Satan plunged Mildred into deep depression, but God was faithful and delivered her. She left a beautiful testimony of God's grace with the psychiatrist. She reduced from two sleeping pills to one and a few weeks later dropped that one and slept better than ever before, and with no withdrawal symptoms.

During those 2½ days I found myself praying with other tongues. This was a tremendous confirmation to me that God was going to bring deliverance. God gave Mildred a prayer language the same week as a confirmation of her baptism of the Spirit. Hallelujah, life hasn't been the same since!

Satan doesn't give up easily. He tried to tell me that this language was gibberish produced by my intense brokenness over Mildred's depressive reaction. I kept rebuking him, but doubts did creep in. Some weeks later I had just finished shaving one morning when I was overwhelmed with an indescribable joy and love and peace and found myself singing and praising God in languages I had never heard before. Beauty and warmth poured down over me, enveloping my whole being. I had heard of others having similar experiences but I thought I had received God's Spirit in a less spectacular way. This came as a precious surprise. I think God knew that my stubborn human mind would keep trying to reason away the evidence, so He just dumped one on me that I couldn't explain away. Praise His name!

All Things Are New

Since His fuller presence is within us, we have had a new awareness of right and wrong. Many things which we formerly accepted as "the way things are" now are seen to be Satan's trap and deceitfulness. The Lord presents us daily with opportunities to witness and He supplies us with the power and the words.

The Bible has become alive and precious and I am daily amazed at all the "new" things He has placed in His Word since He filled us. It is really exciting to have the form of godliness and to know the power thereof. I have learned the reality of Isaiah 59:1, "Behold, the Lord's hand is not shortened, that it cannot save," and of Jeremiah 5:25, "Your iniquities have turned away these things, and your sins have withholden good things from you." I have felt the abundant pardon of Isaiah 55:7.

I know now that God gives his Holy Spirit to those who ask in repentant, obedient faith and that we *shall* receive power when the Holy Spirit comes upon us (Acts 1:8), that "the love of God is shed abroad in our hearts by the Holy Ghost" (Romans 5:5), and that "the law of the Spirit of life in Christ Jesus hath made me free from the law of sin and death" (Romans 8:2).

Our new hunger has prompted us to attend a charismatic fellowship an average of three nights a week. We find the Scripture songs, the opening of the Word, the caring and praying for one another to be a real source of growth. Praise our wonderful Lord!

8
REVITALIZED RETIREMENT
Nelson Litwiller

Who Said We Must Retire at 65?

If anyone had suggested to me that following forty some years on the foreign mission field plus three years in retirement I would be preaching two hundred times a year, I would have shaken my head in doubt. Five years after my wife and I retired we traveled over 50,000 miles in one year, preached on four continents, and have been led into an ample, exciting, and demanding ministry.

I am not trying to set any record. During the last five years, the Lord in His mercy and love has opened many doors of opportunity for preaching and ministry. Ours has been a revitalized retirement. The joy we experience in seeing the Lord confirm the preaching of the Word with signs following cannot be described. Not only are people being saved but individuals are healed. Men and women with emotional problems are touched by the

---

Nelson and Ada Litwiller retired in 1967 after more than forty years of missionary service in Argentina and Uruguay. For many years Nelson was field secretary for Latin America for the Mennonite Board of Missions. The Litwillers are presently Holy Spirit renewal ambassadors at large, traveling frequently to South America and across the length and breadth of North America.

Lord. Scores have entered into a fuller, deeper, and more meaningful relationship with the Lord. I joyfully share our story.

Reared in a Conservative Day

My earliest recollections as a child in Ontario include a multitude of church-related activities. My grandfather was a conservative Amish preacher. Although my father was not a minister, he was vitally interested in everything related to the church. I remember well how grandpa would come across the fields to our home to discuss church problems. The conversations had to do with change. The transition from hooks and eyes to buttons on men's coats, the wearing of neckties, the installation of telephones, the introduction of Sunday schools, night meetings, young people's meetings, and English preaching were all items of tension in our church. The coming of the automobile and the discontinuance of capes, aprons, and bonnets for women were topics of long and serious discussion in the congregation.

Two miles from our home there was a Mennonite church. This group was more tolerant and progressive than ours. Sometimes we attended special revival meetings and three-day Bible conferences with them. This had a good effect on me spiritually. I recall one evening, in such a meeting, that the Holy Spirit spoke to me to yield and put my trust in Jesus. That was more than seventy years ago. But no one expected a child to become a candidate for baptism in our church at that time.

The Appeal of the World and the Call of God

My father was an avid reader and took quite an

interest in public affairs. He would take me along to the
village to listen to the politicians give their campaign
speeches for the federal elections. As a youngster and
hero worshiper I decided that I'd like to become a
politician. To do this I knew I would have to get the
necessary education. High school was frowned upon in
our church in those days. My parents, however, encouraged me and in due time I finished high school and
went on to graduate from a teacher's college. During my
later high school days, after associating with the wrong
crowd for several years, I had a definite conversion
experience at the age of eighteen. Even though I had
been baptized before, my spiritual experience was hazy
and had little significance.

About six months after my conversion, at a missionary
conference, the unmistakable call to foreign missions
came upon my heart. I responded with considerable hesitation and after a genuine inner struggle. I had assumed
mistakenly that to respond meant leaving home at once
to begin a career for which I did not feel prepared and to
which I had given little thought. But I was advised to
complete my training. After finishing teacher's college I
taught public school for a year, married Ada Ramseyer,
and with my companion left Ontario for the United
States and more advanced studies in the fall of 1919.

Early in my high school days, I recall the coming of
Pentecostals to our community. This movement caused
quite a stir among our Amish and Mennonite congregations. The few of our members who became involved
either left the congregation voluntarily, because they no
longer felt welcome, or were excommunicated. As a
youth, even in my unconverted state, I attended some of

their camp meetings out of curiosity. I wasn't too interested and understood little of what was going on. In spite of this, some indelible impressions for good were made on me at the time.

To the Foreign Mission Field

I graduated with a BA degree from Goshen College and a BD degree from Bethany Biblical Seminary in 1925. In the same year, on May 5, Ada and I were appointed and commissioned as missionaries to South America. On June 7, I was ordained to the ministry and we sailed for Buenos Aires, Argentina, on September 5. Nine years had passed from the time of my first call to foreign work to the actual sailing date. In spite of many problems and hurdles which were temptations to discouragement, I could never erase from my heart or conscience the definite call of the Lord to be His ambassador. For this I praise Him.

As a missionary, my career was typical of the time. I was a classical foreigner with high motives, accepted the established methods of the day without much questioning, and dedicated myself to the work with average zeal. I engaged in the accepted activities of evangelistic campaigns, tent crusades, founding congregations, a Bible coach ministry, Bible school work, and administering an orphanage. For ten years I was president of the international Mennonite seminary in Montevideo, Uruguay.

As I grew older, I accepted more responsibility. I was ordained a bishop in the church. Later, I was appointed field secretary of our board for all lower South America. My wife and I enjoyed our work in the several capacities in which we functioned. We rejoice even now for every

triumph in the gospel. We recall with joy the conver-
sions, baptisms, youth meetings, annual conferences, and
retreats with other missionaries and with the nationals in
many countries. I do not wish to minimize in any way
what the Lord accomplished through us during those
years. We have returned to South America since our
retirement with deep satisfaction. To renew acquaintances and friendships and share the things of the
Lord with fellow believers always brings joy.

Envious of the Pentecostals

In traveling to and from in South America as field
secretary it was only natural to meet with other groups. I
learned to know missionaries and leaders of other denominations. I made friends in all the main-line denominations as well as with Pentecostals. Frequently I rejected the latter, not overtly but inwardly. It seemed to
me they manifested an attitude of spiritual superiority.
They looked on us rather condescendingly. Their worship services appeared to us overemotional. Some of the
expressions of worship seemed so exaggerated and in-
consistent with what I was accustomed to that I simply
turned them off.

In all fairness, however, I had to admit that they were
doing good work. Their congregations were growing
faster than those of any other denomination including
our own. I couldn't help but marvel at their extraor-
dinary growth throughout lower South America as well
as in Brazil, Argentina, Chile, Uruguay, and Peru.

It was our privilege to go to South America in 1969 to
help celebrate the fiftieth anniversary of the founding of
a Mennonite witness in Argentina. In central Argentina

in 1969 we had 24 congregations, large and small, 825 communicant members, and six or seven ordained national ministers. A few years before we went to Argentina some charismatic Swedes from Chicago went to Brazil. They had fewer missionaries and even less money than we. The fiftieth anniversary report of our Swedish brethren reads differently. After 50 years they report approximately 840 congregations, nearly 200,000 members, and several hundred ordained men and evangelists. I could repeat examples like this from other countries.

Retirement and Disillusionment

In 1963 we were scheduled to retire. For various reasons this was deferred until 1967. Even though we are Canadian citizens, for family reasons we preferred to settle in the States. To do so it was necessary to continue under the Mission Board until we could qualify to retire on Social Security. In this interim the Board asked us to do deputation work and other special assignments for them. This task took us to many congregations and into many countries.

Our travels and visits to the congregations were varied and sometimes disappointing. Frequently I felt there was lukewarmness, an indifference to spiritual things, worldliness, materialism, and formality. There were internal problems. The brotherhood did not seem closely knit. Unity was missing. In some areas it was almost impossible to get people to come to a prayer meeting. All this distressed me deeply. I prayed much about it. I tried to discover the underlying causes for what seemed to me a spiritual apathy. I was tempted to blame the leadership of the church.

The Lord spoke to me and said, "Why look at others? Look at yourself. You're a leader also!" A great sense of inadequacy came over me as the Spirit helped me to do some real soul searching. More and more I felt keenly that my own relationship with the Lord was not as intimate and full and free as it should be.

Overwhelmed with Inadequacy

Early in 1970 the Mission Board asked us to do another stint for them in Europe. We assented gladly, but as the summer dragged on my sense of inadequacy grew more intense. I didn't feel I had what it took. We almost abandoned the idea of going. I felt that my career was finished. I had made my contribution. There was nothing more that I could do.

As I reflected on my life's work, I felt that the harvest had been rather slim. In spite of many things for which I could be grateful, I was also painfully conscious that the fruit of the Spirit had been rather seasonal in my life. I had time to reflect and compare notes. I was 72 years old and had almost concluded, "This is it. You've had it. It's time to retire indeed and not get involved in anything more from here on out."

But the Lord knows when we come to the end of ourselves. He is near when we reach point zero. His love never abandons us. Several things happened almost simultaneously. A friend gave me the book, *Catholic Pentecostals*, by Kevin and Dorothy Ranaghan. What was going on in the Catholic Church interested me intensely for I had known them for fifty years. What I read in this book was news. About the same time the headlines in the *Elkhart Truth* announced in bold letters,

"Catholic Pentecostals Close Conference." I remarked, "Why do they tell a fellow when they close the conference and not when they open it!"

Made Hungry by the Roman Catholics

Professor John Howard Yoder, of the Associated Mennonite Biblical Seminaries in Elkhart, Indiana, heard me make this remark. He sensed my interest and gave me the names of Dr. Edward O'Connor and Professor Kevin Ranaghan and suggested I see them. Almost at the same time a brother and sister, neighbors of ours at Greencroft Retirement Community in Goshen, Indiana, invited me to come with them to a prayer meeting in South Bend.

They took me on a hot humid night in June. I didn't know of a single place in all northern Indiana where ten people would gather for a midweek prayer meeting. To my amazement I found some 120 people in the gymnasium of St. Joseph's parochial high school in South Bend. Nuns, priests, professors and their wives, students from the university, businessmen, professionals, Catholics and Protestants, were praising God together, worshiping, rejoicing, singing, testifying to the goodness of the Lord. They were sincerely thanking Jesus for His love and blessings. I could hardly believe my eyes and ears. I had known the Catholics in South America but had never seen anything like this. Here there was a dimension of joy and praise and fellowship in a dynamic and spontaneous manner that I had never witnessed before. Here I found all the elements of group worship, sharing, and fellowship without the excesses for which I had faulted Pentecostals consistently for years.

I returned to the South Bend prayer meeting the

second week and the third. During this time I prayed and fasted as I had never done before and asked the Lord to search my heart. My great sense of inadequacy continued. On my third visit to the prayer meeting, I was moved to share with someone my deep need for more power in my life. I was invited to a classroom upstairs for special prayer. Six or seven of us gathered in a small circle. We were told that we should look to the Lord and ask Him to meet our needs.

A group of four or five laid hands on me. The leader prayed that I might be delivered from doubt and pride and fear of the people. I didn't know that I needed deliverance. I was not aware of being bound in any way. But here I was, and they were praying for me, I reflected. Then, in an instant, the Holy Spirit revealed my whole life to me as on a screen. I saw Nelson Litwiller as I had never seen myself before. The searchlight of the Spirit was focused on my inner being. I became aware of pride, selfishness, anxiety, and fear. I saw that I had been seeking success and popularity. (For one can be a preacher and seek praise for oneself rather than sincerely endeavoring to glorify Jesus.) I covered a lot of ground in a short time as I was going through this spiritual crisis.

The Lord spoke clearly to me. "Will you make an absolute, unqualified, unconditional surrender in a way that you have never done before? Will you yield everything to me?" In my innermost being, as well as I knew how, I said, "Yes, Lord." I admit this is a humiliating confession for an ex-missionary to make. But the moment I said, "Yes, Lord," something unusual happened. I was delivered from doubt and reticence and fear of the people. I could not have cared less what others thought.

An unusual dimension of peace and joy filled my being. In the words of Peter, I had joy unspeakable and full of glory.

I was not looking particularly for any special manifestation. As I started to praise the Lord with overflowing joy, strange syllables and words came to my mind and tongue. I was praising the Lord in a strange language. I repeat, I was not looking for this experience. I was given no instructions or orientation regarding tongues. As I praised the Lord in my unspeakable joy, those who had prayed for me laughed heartily and moved on.

Strange to say, I cannot remember what happened after that. I assume they prayed for the others in the circle. When I got outside, the neighbors who had taken me to the meeting were waiting in their car. They remarked that it seemed to them that the Lord had touched me. This I affirmed. They said, "When the Lord baptized us in the Spirit, we wanted to share our experience with everyone else. We tried to push our experience down everybody's throat, and they resented it. Don't make the same mistake."

"Thank you," I said. "That's good advice. If my wife can't see a different husband, if the people for whom I preach can't hear a different preacher, then there's no use in my telling them." I wasn't going to hide my light under a bushel but neither was I going to twist anyone's arm or be a bore.

Refurbished for Service

Ten days later we were off to Europe to minister to Spanish-speaking migrants in the industrial area of the

northern European countries. But the Lord gave me an
added assignment. In meeting and fellowshiping with
Christian workers in several countries, the Lord opened
the door for me to share and witness to my deeper
experience. Tremendous things happened and have been
happening ever since. People with physical, emotional,
and spiritual problems have been touched and restored
to wholeness. I say all this to the honor and gloryof Jesus.
I believe that divine healing is only one method of God's
intervention. In no way would I disparage the way God
works through doctors, psychiatrists, counselors, and
nurses. I believe that anyone who prays for healing
should have a healthy respect for all other types of healing.

The Apostle Paul says that the kingdom of God is not a
matter of words but of power. I felt that for too long I
had made the kingdom a matter of words. There was not
the corresponding manifestation of power. Jesus' promise
to His disciples was, "You will receive power." This is a
power not only to witness but to minister.

Let me state emphatically that I do not claim moral or
spiritual superiority to anyone. Nor do I claim that a
deeper spiritual experience in the Holy Spirit has made
me a better Christian than others. Nor am I interested in
any way in becoming a part of a pressure group or
separatist movement within the church. I must, however,
testify to the fact that my experience in the Holy Spirit
has made me a happier Christian and more effective
minister than I was before. And I rejoice in this as a work
of unmerited grace of my Savior and Lord Jesus Christ.

I believe the Lord in His mercy allowed me this touch
not only for my own sake. I believe He wants me to share

this simple yet profound reality with believers everywhere. And especially to all my colleagues and pastors, called to the ministry, I should like to give a word of encouragement. Do you long for a joyful and meaningful and fruitful ministry? I suggest that among other things the indispensable requirement for an effective ministry is to be filled with the Spirit of God. I believe it is necessary to give the Holy Spirit full freedom in my life and allow the gifts of the Spirit to operate freely. A Spirit-filled ministry will be an overflowing and contagious ministry. And this will touch and strengthen the entire brotherhood, the body of Christ.

9

I'M JUST A TEENAGER, BUT I LOVE JESUS

Karen Roes

Wonders and Signs

"Praise the Lord, Karen! We knew the Lord would heal you and bless you."

The words of my father still echo in my ears. I was one of those kids who went to church every Sunday and, although I was by no means an angel, I was not the black sheep in the church.

I was brought up in a Christian home in Ontario and was saved at an early age. I was to learn in several years about a God who abundantly took care of His children, blessing them and healing them.

My great-aunt and her husband were God's instruments in getting the ball rolling in our family. Great-Aunt Erma had a serious back condition which caused severe pain when she walked and especially when she bent over. Eventually she was confined to a wheelchair. But the Lord touched her body and her spirit. I remember the night they first told us about her healing. I

Karen Roes is the oldest daughter of Mahlon and Pearl Roes of Milverton, Ontario. Interested in music, she is a member of the Crosshill Mennonite Church.

kept saying to myself, "Wow, God! You did this?"

My parents were intrigued by this most unusual healing and tried to find out more about it. Within a year,
they opened their hearts to the Lord in a fresh way and
received the baptism of the Holy Spirit.

When I first heard of Daddy receiving the gift of
tongues, I said, "That's nice, but you can have it. I don't
need it." I had no burning desire for the baptism.

"Jesus 73" Did It for Me

Mother and Daddy and I started to attend Full Gospel
Business Men's breakfasts in Toronto. The people at
those meetings seemed to have the abundant life and joy
unspeakable that is talked about in the Word of God.
How I wanted the joy that everyone there demonstrated!
Joy just bubbled out of those people.

In the summer of 1973, a girl friend of mine invited
my younger sister and brother and me to go to a "Jesus
73," a Christian camp-out in Pennsylvania, to hear some
good speakers. We decided we had nothing to lose, so
why not?

I had a rash all over my legs from an allergy to buffalo
hide sandals. The rash was so bad that my legs were completely infected and looked horrible. The itching was in-
tolerable. Whenever I was exposed to sunlight for more
than ten or fifteen minutes, my legs would feel as if they
were burning up. That's the condition I was in when our
crowded school bus finally arrived at "Jesus 73" in
Pennsylvania after a long, thirteen-hour drive.

The attitude of everyone really amazed me. People I
had never met before greeted me with "Praise the Lord"
and "Hallelujah." Wow!

From nine o'clock in the morning to 12:00 midnight, 12,000 people worshiped and listened to the Word of God. The whole experience was beautiful. I had never seen so many people with their hands raised in adoration. I wanted so bad to worship in spirit and truth too, so I raised my hands and asked the Lord to fill me up to overflowing with His Spirit, His joy, His love, and His peace. Hallelujah! He did it!

He set me free. He took away those burdens I had been hanging on to. I wanted to praise Him like I never had before. I was baptized in a little creek along with 2,000 other people. I came up out of the water feeling clean and, oh, so pure in Him.

For the first time in my life I saw that the Father wants our praise. He desires to inhabit our praises.

Jesus Still Can Quiet a Storm

One night during the meeting, clouds began to darken the sky. Since no one wanted rain, the speakers prayed that a big wind would blow the clouds away. Well, it got windy! God's children who were there started to praise Him. With every thunder and flash of lightning the people praised God.

It rained but no one really cared. The shower refreshed our bodies after two days of 90-degree temperatures. We all joined in singing:

Jesus, Jesus, Jesus' There's just something about that name.
Jesus, Jesus, Jesus; like the fragrance after the rain.
Jesus, Jesus, Jesus; let all heaven and earth proclaim,
Kings and kingdoms will all pass away,
Yet there's something about that name.

Jesus was that fragrance after the rain.

Then we heard the most exciting news. Three state troopers had been watching the storm. They saw a tornado coming straight toward our crowd. Then it made an unaccountable turn and went around the campground. That was the Lord taking care of us. (P.S. The troopers were saved.)

I Was Healed, Praise God!

The next to last night of that great meeting I decided to go to the prayer tent for healing. My legs were itching furiously because they had been exposed to sunlight for a long time. Someone prayed for me and the Lord started the healing.

The next morning the scabs started to fall off. On the way home I felt the itching again. Geraldine, my girl friend's mother, said she would pray with me. She told me to thank God for the healing. I did, and all of a sudden I was praying in my new prayer language. I asked for one thing and the Lord blessed me with another.

My parents were overjoyed when I told them what happened to me. All they could say was, "Praise the Lord, Karen," and "Thank You, Lord!" They said they *knew* the Lord would heal and bless me.

Those three days at "Jesus 73" were beautiful, but they were just the beginning of the good things God had in store for me. The Lord doesn't want us to live on other people's experiences, miracles, and healings. He wants us to have our own.

Abundant Life Continues

In the 3½ years that have gone by since I came to

know the Lord in this deeper way, I have learned so much. In July 1975 we had an Abundant Life Conference in Stratford, Ontario, similar to "Renewal 74" and "Renewal 75." My father was cochairman of the conference and so we were involved in the organization. I knew that God wanted the conference just by the way things worked together. The sense of unity that prevailed was in itself a beautiful working of God.

I found out that Mennonites over 30 love Jesus too. As pianist, I was asked to sit on the platform with the speakers and the committee. The love and adoration that everyone expressed to Jesus was very moving. Hands and voices were raised to magnify the one name—Jesus.

The Lord has brought our family much closer together than we were before. Although we are sometimes scattered at a distance from each other physically, our family is knit together closely in the Spirit of the Lord. My father and mother are two beautiful people, and I praise God for the way He is using them.

Daddy is president of the Stratford chapter of the Full Gospel Business Men's Fellowship International. My sisters and brother, all younger than myself, have come into a beautiful relationship with the Father also.

The Lord has led many beautiful committed people together. I attend a gathering of His people every Friday night known as the Jacob's Well Fellowship. At this fellowship several hundred people come to minister to the Lord in praise and to be ministered to by His Word. I praise Him for the brothers and sisters in the Lord I have there and elsewhere. Their love and the love of my own family and special friends have really blessed me richly. Hallelujah!

The Lord has done much for me and continues to discipline me in love. Without His perfect timing and His perfect love, I would be nothing. In Him I can live abundantly. Praise God!

"When the Spirit of truth comes, he will guide you into all the truth; for he will not speak on his own authority, but whatever he hears he will speak, and he will declare to you the things that are to come. He will glorify me, for he will take what is mine and declare it to you" (John 16:13, 14).

"God is spirit, and those who worship him must worship in spirit and truth" (John 4:24).

10

HE BLESSES, AND BLESSES, AND BLESSES AGAIN!

James and Beatrice Hess

James Shares

In December of 1974 Nelson Litwiller, a missionary retired from the field in South America, came to our congregation for a week of meetings. Nelson was widely known for his interest and activity in the charismatic movement. I had met him first in Bogota, Colombia, in 1968.

In Bogota I had seen Pentecostal excesses in a local church which had caused me to reject glossolalia as not being of the Lord. That was some years before. Since that time the Lord had showed me that by the same reasoning I could reject salvation as the work of God because some who are at one time truly saved later turn back to the world. I could reject the Lord's call to the ministry, for I have known ministers of the gospel who made shipwreck of their lives. I could reject the church,

---

James and Beatrice Hess were missionaries in Honduras for nineteen years under the Eastern Mennonite Mission Board. James is pastor of the East Chestnut Street Mennonite Church, Lancaster, Pennsylvania. Earlier he was Employment Supervisor in a New Holland, Pennsylvania, industry.

for I have found no perfect group of people who call themselves the church of Christ.

In those meetings Nelson told us about the baptism with the Holy Spirit. He talked about new peace and power and tongues and prophecy. He encouraged us to ask for God's blessings that accompany the Holy Spirit's infilling. We pondered and hesitated.

Praise God, He doesn't get hung up over our imperfections and inconsistencies and hesitation. He just says, "Look, don't keep trying to serve Me in your own strength. If I have called you and commissioned you, don't you think I can enable you too? I have all the resources you need, all the abundant, perfect love you crave in a world of hate. Just hold out your hands in faith. I will fill them. You are a father. You wouldn't give your children anything that is harmful to them when they ask for something good, would you? Then why shouldn't I give you the Holy Spirit when you ask Me?"

Finally we asked. Late one evening Beatrice and I, and Wilbur and Romaine Miller, met with Nelson and Ada Litwiller in our living room to do business with God. Nelson prayed going from person to person. All of us prayed and praised.

I told the Lord that I am ready for all He wishes to give me. I tried to shove aside my past prejudices, but I must confess that in a little recess of my mind I still harbored a bit of prejudice against glossolalia.

But God smiled down upon us that midnight hour. His love immersed us. Our praises ascended to His holy hill. All our fears were washed away. Pure joy spilled from our overflowing hearts. We exalted Jesus in our lives as never before.

God Was Leading Us in Grace

God had all these blessings in mind for us many years earlier, even before Beatrice and I knew each other. In the Conestoga Valley of Lancaster County, Pennsylvania, and in the Shenandoah Valley of Rockingham County, Virginia, a young boy and girl early in life gave their hearts to the Savior. God sealed them with the Holy Spirit of promise to the praise of His glory. We had no special claim on the Lord for our guidance, but the Lord did have His claim on us.

God led our lives together in a beautiful way. He gave me convictions to serve Him on the mission field. I discovered that God was working similarly in the life of lovely Beatrice.

Even before we were married the veteran church statesman, Henry Garber, asked us to serve the church in Honduras. We accepted this challenge as the confirmation of the desire the Lord had already put into our hearts to serve Him in overseas missions.

We really didn't have a good way to verbalize all that the Lord was doing for us, but God didn't ask for that. We knew that the Father had saved us by His grace. His Spirit had applied Christ's redemptive work in our hearts. Now He was asking us to step out in obedient faith and He would guide us step by step when the time came.

To the Mission Field and Back

Nineteen years in a land of *mañana* were years of sharing, growing, learning, doing and undoing, frustrations, victories, and continual yielding to God who patiently guided and molded us after the image of His dear Son.

At times that image was distorted, we must confess, and many times the molding process was slow.

But praise God! His patience, love, and persistence in the good work He had begun in us was not thwarted by our failures. He reminded us that we can always come back and receive the forgiveness and renewal that is so abundantly poured out on us by His grace.

After nearly twenty years on the mission field, what does a couple do upon returning to the routine of Stateside life, with the probability of at least another twenty years of active life before us?

The Lord led me to a job with a local industry. He led Beatrice to a position as bookkeeper in a Christian day school. Both of these positions have made possible further training and molding of our lives for God's purposes. We agreed with William Cowper when he said of God's leading, "His purposes will ripen fast, unfolding every hour." This has been true in our experiences.

Thank the Lord that He is not static, nor does He let us stalemate. Had we continued for fifty years in Honduras, we're sure His purposes would have unfolded as He revealed them day by day and hour by hour.

Called to Pastor My Home Church

In 1973 I was called to serve as assistant pastor of the East Chestnut Street Mennonite Church in Lancaster, Pennsylvania. It was this congregation that had first established a Mennonite witness in Honduras in 1950. To be the assistant pastor was a very convenient arrangement for us because it permitted me to continue my employment in the personnel department of the local industry. My pastoral duties required only occasional preaching and minimal visitation.

But it wasn't long until the congregation began speaking of the need for a full-time pastor. In meetings of the church council and of the congregation the matter was discussed at length and the Lord's will was sought in prayer. Occasionally someone asked me the question, "Would you accept the call to full-time pastoral responsibility if the Lord so leads?"

I was always evasive and tried to suggest that I would be happy to continue under the present arrangement. But I never really had peace about that answer. It was a rational reply but not really a word from the Lord.

In their further search to find God's will, the congregation's leaders suggested that all who could should set aside a day for prayer and fasting before giving nominations. Roy Koch, who was a guest speaker at "Renewal 74" in nearby Landisville, preached for the congregation a sermon that pointed out the necessary qualifications for pastoral leadership. The following Sunday nominations were to be taken.

On Friday, two days before the nominations were to be submitted, I took a vacation day from work and struggled most of the day with the Lord. I knew then that I would be called, and I was resisting the Lord's leading. I wrestled with God in prayer. And praise His holy name! He touched my spirit so that my walk was not lame but firm and in confidence. That Sunday morning the Lord gave us great peace as the bishops confirmed to the congregation its call for us to serve them.

God Is So Good

We have seen God's hand of protection and blessing

upon us all the way through our lives. We stand in awe and wonder at His marvelous goodness over the years.

Beatrice was hit and run over by a truck at the age of six. A drunk pointed a loaded revolver at the side of my head from two feet away and pulled the trigger three times without its going off. Two of our sons escaped uninjured from the cab of a pickup that was crushed like an accordion by the wing of a large plane that had lost its brakes in landing. Another son survived a night of continuous breathing stoppage and lapses into unconsciousness. In all these things, God was showing us that His hand was upon us for good.

During these many years since, the Father has been revealing more and more of His purpose in our lives. To Him be all the glory.

God Remains Our Unfailing Strength

And what has it been like since the Lord anointed that quartet in our living room at midnight? Are we living on cloud nine? No, not really. It seems more like cloud 999! Just one level under millennium bliss! But that level contains all my weaknesses and shortcomings. It's just that now my weaknesses don't dominate my life; Jesus is the predominate One. When I awake in the middle of the night with a problem facing me, I praise the Lord and the problem is not the mountain it appeared to be. When I experience deep anxiety of soul after hearing of another Christian's defeats, I praise the Lord that He has the solution, and joy replaces dread. The Lord makes the rough places plain. The valleys are exalted, the mountains are made low, and the glory of the Lord is revealed.

I am humbled by God's blessings in my life through

Christ, for I did nothing but say, "Yes, Lord." then He blessed and blesses, and I know He will continue to bless for His good purposes. In all honesty, I can say with the wise man, "The blessing of the Lord makes rich, and he adds no sorrow with it" (Proverbs 10:22).

Beatrice Shares

One busy Saturday morning I felt a sudden pain in my back. It was as though something slipped out of place. I had instant pain. Two days later the pain was so intense that we went to see the doctor.

A week of treatment did not relieve the pain, but it did relieve our pocketbooks. I was discouraged. X-rays did not help my spirits a bit. The doctor said, "You have two horses hitched to the cart instead of one—a herniated disc and a buildup of arthritis on the spine. So it will probably mean hospitalization with traction or surgery." Medication relieved the pain, but at the same time it made me so dizzy it was difficult for me to perform my duties.

Then came Renewal 74 the last weekend of May. Renewal 74 was a charismatic churchwide conference held at Landisville, Pennsylvania, just a few miles from our home. When James mentioned something about attending the meetings I recoiled at first. But at the same time something within me seemed to say, "Perhaps something wonderful will happen to me there."

I decided to attend the healing workshop taught by Fred Augsburger. At first the odds were against us. We had to sit in the back near the door because we were a bit late in arriving. Also I had a restless daughter who preferred to be outside rather than inside.

At the close of the class period I was sure that Fred would say he felt impelled by the Lord to minister to someone with a back ailment. But he didn't. Instead he called for someone with a neck problem to claim the healing. Two individuals raised their hands and Fred prayed for them.

Then he gave the invitation for persons present to raise their hands if they had other afflictions and desired healing. Oh, joy! Up went my hand. Because of where we were sitting, James was the closest person to lay hands on me while Fred prayed. While he was praying I felt the warmth of the Lord's touch. His love flowed through my body and removed the pain. I felt like walking and leaping and praising God as we left that building.

I realized that God had given me more than I had asked for. Beside a physical healing He healed me spiritually as well. Isn't that like the blessed Savior? He always gives us more than we ask for. Now I knew how those people felt when the Lord healed them and also added, "Thy sins be forgiven thee."

It seemed that Jesus had been right there and touched me and I knew it was for real, although I didn't say anything to James since Fred had warned that if any were on medication they should continue and not drop it until advised by the doctor to do so. I did stop taking pills, however, and have not taken one since. That was more than a year ago.

Jesus Solves Our Problems

In God's school of life there are many lessons to learn. Some of His lessons are painful. While we were on the mission field in Honduras there were times when we

would dream with stars in our eyes of the day when we
would own a house of our own and earn a salary instead
of a monthly allowance.

This dream became a reality several years ago when
the Lord indicated to us that the time had come to
remain in the United States with our children instead of
returning to the mission field.

We built our own house which was now our home. We
had fruit trees and a garden. James' employment was all
he could ask for, and I rejoiced daily in a Christian school
atmosphere with my fingers busy on the typewriter and
working with figures.

Then came the call to serve at the East Chestnut Street
Mennonite Church. That would mean giving up some
things, and we rebelled. The Lord began to deal with
me. He was saying tenderly, "Aren't my benefits better
than any company's? They will pay expenses, but I heal.
Don't be afraid to be on my payroll. I'll take care of your
needs."

Thus the fire began to burn in my heart until it was a
big bonfire. Into that fire went the house, job, benefits,
and what have you. And when only smoldering embers
remained, I could say, "Lord, I'll live anywhere and I'll
give up everything."

And then came praise—praise for healing, praise for
joy, peace, and a new song in my heart. And as I praised,
James' was ready to say "Yes" to whatever the Lord had
for us.

Things started happening in our family. It seemed the
windows of heaven were opened and the blessings
poured down. James was 2,000 miles away in Honduras
to help after the destruction of Hurricane Fifi. As I

prayed about a house located closer to Lancaster for our work, I asked the Lord to take care of financing that house. He found us the house and the finances for it. Praise the Lord,

We are still praising Him. Heaven is more real, prayer, Bible reading, and fellowship have all taken on a new dimension.

Each day is like heaven, my heart overflows.
The longer I serve Him the sweeter He grows.

11

FALSE STARTS AND THEN THE GENUINE

Edward and Ethel Miller

Into the Ministry Unprepared

Probably few persons have been catapulted into the gospel ministry as unprepared as I was. I was born and raised Amish. In 1942, during World War II, I was drafted and assigned as a conscientious objector to a project at Luray, Virginia. There I was saved by reading and believing Ephesians 2:8, 9, when I discovered that salvation is a gift. I thought that took care of my spiritual needs, but a number of years later I discovered that God had some additional delights for me in Ephesians.

Soon after I was saved, and just before transferring to Gulfport, Mississippi, to help open a new Civilian Public Service (CPS) camp, I joined the Mennonite Church at Plain City, Ohio. Following 3½ years of CPS, I spent eighteen months in Voluntary Service (VS) also at Gulfport. During this VS period I was ordained as associate

---

Edward and Ethel Miller live in Grand Rapids, Michigan, where he pastors the North Park Mennonite Church. They have also served the Glennon Heights Mennonite Church, Denver, Colorado, and the Wayside and Gulfhaven Mennonite churches, Gulfport, Mississippi. Edward was born at Hartville, Ohio; Ethel comes from Lancaster, Pennsylvania.

pastor of the Gulfhaven Mennonite Church. Soon after my ordination, I met Ethel Eby, who became my wife and shared the years of my ministry with me.

About a year after my ordination I was released from my charge at Gulfhaven to start the Wayside Mission Church, just north of the city. I knew that I was saved, and I was zealous in outreach work for the Lord, but I was laboring under the bondage of legalism, and without formal training. I felt a deep hunger for more of God, often praying long hours into the night. I felt the need for teaching on the Spirit and how one receives Him.

I Gave God All I Had

Then we heard of the Brunk Brothers tent meetings in the East, and that George R. Brunk was giving altar calls specifically for receiving the fullness of the Holy Spirit. My heart leaped with anticipation. A carload of delightful young men whose lives had been greatly altered as a result of their encounter with God at the Brunk meetings came to our home in Gulfport. Their testimonies created an even greater hunger within me.

When I learned that our district conference was scheduled to be held on the Hutchinson, Kansas, fairgrounds in conjunction with the Brunk Brothers revival meetings conducted in a big tent, I knew I must go. I sensed, as did my wife and others who were seeking with me, that the hunger we felt had to do with the Holy Spirit.

At those meetings Brother Brunk preached on the scriptural conditions for receiving the Holy Spirit. He explained that, as Christ is received by accepting Calvary by faith, so the Holy Spirit is received by accepting

Pentecost by faith. He gave seekers an opportunity to act upon that faith by responding to an altar call. I have never responded as eagerly as I did that evening in the tent when I went forward to receive a fuller work of the Holy Spirit in my life.

I returned to Gulfport, to my family, and to my congregation feeling completely new inside. I preached and witnessed with a new joy and liberty that was noticeable to my family and my flock at Wayside. I knew that the glowing testimonies and the higher level of victory in me and in others resulted from my new experience with the Holy Spirit.

Detoured by the Fear of Man

But testings and discouragement followed. I experienced personal confusion when I began hearing of incompatibility and divisions among those I was looking up to. I felt alone, having no one to teach me how to walk in the Spirit. I entered a period of disenchantment with the entire new emphasis on the Holy Spirit.

In the several years that followed I must have deeply grieved and thoroughly quenched the Spirit repeatedly, for I steadfastly resisted Him. I deliberately avoided mentioning Him in my preaching and teaching lest I become identified with those who seemed to thrive on being dramatic and were trying to outdo one another in special manifestations of the Holy Spirit.

Yet I knew that something was also wrong with me. How could I go on ignoring the Holy Spirit in my preaching when He is mentioned so frequently in the Bible? I was being hypocritical and untrue to the Word of God. I remembered also something that George R. Brunk had said, "I know that there is counterfeit money in circulation, but I'm not about to throw away all the money in my billfold." This helped me to realize that if there are misuses of the Spirit there must also be a relationship to Him that is real and genuine!

I began once more in my preaching and teaching to mention the Holy Spirit and His importance in the Christian life. But I was not myself filled with the Spirit to the point where I was under His control. Again I was hungry and thirsty. I deeply desired to be filled with the Spirit, to understand more about what He could do in my life, and to be taught in a fellowship with others who shared the same concerns.

On the Right Track at Last

By this time I was pastoring the Glennon Heights congregation in Denver, Colorado. There a group of us came together to seek the Holy Spirit. This developed into a house fellowship. I was among them, not as the pastor, but as a fellow seeker. Several times one, or two, or more of this fellowship reported receiving the Spirit at another church, or at home alone, in a variety of places and ways.

One evening some guests were with us to share their experiences and to teach us more about the Holy Spirit. I found answers to a number of questions that freed me from some hang-ups I had developed over the years. As the group was joining hands in prayer, I felt strongly urged to ask our teachers, Ed Gregory, associated with the Billy Graham team, and Ed Richardson, an associate pastor at Calvary temple, to lay hands upon me that I might receive the Holy Spirit in His fullness.

I knelt. A loving, caring, sharing group gathered

around me and laid hands upon me and Ethel, who knelt beside me. Several prayed, and I prayed. I simply accepted the outpouring of Pentecost by faith. Suddenly, for the first time in my life, I heard spontaneous singing in the Spirit. Several in our group, for whom this was previously unheard of, were participating. It was the most beautiful music I had ever heard, although I could understand none of the words. All were individually singing in a language the Spirit gave them.

Aside from the loveliness and sacredness of the moment, I personally felt no different than before. I took Ethel to work for the night shift at the hospital. Then I returned home.

When I was alone in my bedroom, the Spirit came upon me with an urge to speak the Word. Scriptures rushed to my mind. I found myself speaking them, singing them, and praising the Lord with them. How long this continued, I do not know. I finally retired, but I don't know if I really slept with vivid dreaming, or if I was awake with impressions from the Holy Spirit. Whatever the case, it was joyful, delightful, and simply wonderful!

All night long, and after I awoke in the morning, fantastic, continuous music surged through my mind. Songs of long ago returned to my lips. All I wanted to do was sing. I went to my study at the church. Until nearly noon I sang and sang, by memory, from the hymnal, and improvising as the Spirit enabled me. There was no unknown tongue. I understood every word I was uttering, but I did not fully understand what was happening.

Later that forenoon I recalled the phrase, "Singing and making melody in your heart to the Lord." I said to myself, "That's Scripture. But where is it found?" *Cruden's Complete Concordance* led me to Ephesians 5:19. As my eyes roamed over the setting of that verse, my heart leaped with recognition of what had been happening to me. Ephesians 5:18, which obviously precedes verse 19, had my answer. "Be not drunk with wine, wherein is excess; but be filled with the Spirit; speaking to yourselves in psalms and hymns and spiritual songs, singing and making melody in your heart to the Lord."

I had received the infilling—the baptism—the coming upon—of the Holy Spirit! And it was confirmed by a special manifestation, not of tongues, but by singing and melody in my heart that for me was supernatural.

Free in the Spirit

Since that glorious event, I have continued to experience an abiding presence, a constant joy, a new dimension of assurance. Testings and trials still assail me, but always His comforting presence is there, deep within. For me the baptism in the Spirit has not merely added something new to my life. It has released me from the old burdens, cares, and problems that otherwise would have overwhelmed me and caused me to give up my pastoral and preaching ministry.

When I was a young Amish boy, I could hardly wait until the cold of winter had passed and I could shed my long, heavy underwear and run barefoot through the new grass. How free and unencumbered I felt. How much fun it was to run! This is the sensation of freedom I have felt since the Spirit has been released within me.

Space does not permit me to tell of my hang-ups and the things I had to learn more correctly before I was

ready to let the Holy Spirit have His way in my life. But
one major truth the Lord revealed to me became a real
turning point in my life. He showed me that all the warnings I had ever heard regarding the hassles, divisions,
and problems associated with a visitation of the Holy
Spirit—all these negative ideas come from men, and not
from God.

I discovered that in His Holy Word, where God mentions the Holy Spirit countless times, not a single warn-
ing is given against the Holy Spirit, not one case where
He brought division, jealousy, or pride. He is always
mentioned as a good, holy, desirable, positive factor in
the Christian's life. The only warnings concerning the
Holy Spirit are directed to God's people: don't grieve
don't quench, and don't resist the Holy Spirit!

I hesitated to respond to the request that I submit my
experiences with the Holy Spirit to this volume for fear
that I would seek personal glory or imply that I am superior to others in any way. Those who know me best are
aware of my lack of perfection and of total sanctification.
I claim neither. I desire both.

I do know of a certainty that my Savior, Jesus Christ,
has by the infilling of the Holy Spirit given me the
Comforter. Now I have an additional resource for doing
battle with self and Satan. I have entered a new level of
love, joy, and peace in the Holy Spirit. Ethel has
experienced this new infilling with me. We have enjoyed
a new sense of wonderful marriage unity, sharing deeply
our innermost feelings, weeping, praying, and laughing
together in a growing oneness and deepening love for
each other.

Ethel did not intend to share her experience in this

volume, but I have intercepted a letter which she wrote recently to a young lady in which she gives her frank testimony. With her consent, I include her testimony with mine. It confirms in my own heart what I have observed in her at close range. (Only the name of the addressee is changed.)

Dear Debbie:

I identify closely with you, Debbie, in that part of your letter where you said you just cry and cry inside. Debbie, God has something much better than that for you! There are all these verses about constant joy. Then why don't you have this constant joy? I think it may be because you are a child of God, but apparently you are not walking in the Spirit.

I speak from my own experience. I was a Christian over thirty years. I had no problems to speak of as a youth. God was good to me and I was happy in the Lord. I tried only to be acceptable to Him and didn't worry about making an impression on any person. Then God gave me a good, loving, Christian husband and four precious children.

I took my nurse's training and helped my husband earn for our home before we had children, and then again after they were all in school. They never had a baby-sitter, and I thought I was sharing and teaching them about the true God and real life.

Things Got Very Bad

But gradually my world shattered. I cried all the time, either inside or outside. Even in church, yes especially in church, I could hardly keep from crying. Our three sons turned against us and against God. I had to live with cursing, smoking, drinking, filthy magazines, cynicism, anger, and rock music day after day in my own home. I couldn't imagine how it happened. John, our youngest as you know, was too small to be a part of it.

We got telephone calls from the police at night. I seemed to be living in Satan's house. Why? Oh, why? What could I do? Nothing! I prayed, and I cried. I explained. Nothing helped. I watched helplessly as things got worse. The two older boys deliberately took the third son into their way.

I was brokenhearted and angry. Where was God and justice? Then when I was about to crack up, when it was bad enough that I asked for help, when I had no pride left in myself, then I was willing, in fact, I had to ask for help. A friend had called a small group together for our first house fellowship. Only about a dozen people were present at that meeting. But they were "the church," my spiritual family.

I Was Healed by the Spirit of God

Three young people told simply how they had gone to Redeemer Temple and had received the baptism of the Holy Spirit that week. I knew about the Holy Spirit and had asked for the baptism before. But this time I had other problems. Right then they were so bad that I told the group about my children and asked them to gather around me and lay hands on me and pray for my emotional healing. Now, remember, I had never before been in a meeting where anyone had done this. From this I learned that we can minister to each other, and God performs miracles.

People cannot pray for you if you don't share your hurts with them. You need Christians you can be close to. That night someone called my attention to Romans 5:5 in *The Living Bible* which says, "We are able to hold our heads high no matter what happens and know that all is well, for we know how dearly God loves us, and we feel this warm love everywhere within us because God has given us the Holy Spirit to fill our hearts with his love."

I went home and started feeding on that verse. I didn't feel any miracle changing me at the meeting that evening, but it happened quietly, like snow melting. The next day I realized I was healed! God took away all the hurts and anger and self-pity, and instead I just loved my boys. And all the crying was gone. Really! I could hardly believe it then, and it overwhelms me even now. How I thank the Lord! Imagine, no more crying inside, just love and laughing! And singing—my heart was singing to Jesus! Suddenly I could pray all the time, and now it was with joy instead of crying.

The whole situation was clearer than ever in my mind. I didn't condone evil, but I did love everybody. The problems with my sons got much, much worse. But even then I could live right in it, feeling sorry for them, yet loving them without feeling loved by them in return. In a sense, I was untouched, undefeated, by what went on around me. The difference was in that I was learning to walk in the Spirit.

With the Spirit in me, I can be an island of peace and joy and love no matter what swirls around me. I don't know when I first received the Spirit, but I ask every day and often during each day, for Jesus to fill me with His Spirit. It is continuing as a constant thing, both the pray-

ing and the loving. Certainly I have never been perfect
in this, but whenever I feel a lack of joy, a constant inner
moping and crying, I confess it as sin and ask again to be
filled with the Spirit and for Him to please restore the
joy. When I sense a lack of love for even one person, I
confess it as sin, and ask to be refilled with the peace the
Spirit gives.

Now I Have a Ministry of Comfort

The years have gone by. Things have changed a little.
The boys no longer live with us. I believe our third son
loves us, and the older ones probably do too, a little, but
they are still living in the camp of the enemy. I pray day
and night for their salvation. I also pray for the constant
fullness of the Spirit for myself, and that I'll have
patience, gentleness, meekness, kindness—all the fruit of
the Spirit!

Go over in your mind the fruit of the Spirit in Galatians
5:22, 23. Notice also verses 25 and 26, and if you lack any
of the qualities mentioned, ask for the Spirit to fill you
and give you that which you lack. You've been born into
Christ's family by the Spirit. Now learn to walk in the
Spirit. You were born a baby. Now you are maturing.
The Bible teaches us to die to self daily and that means
confessing these things as sin. As Sherwood Wirt puts it,
"You are a glass full of cloudy, dirty, water. Empty it out
so God can pour in His sparkling, clear water of the Holy
Spirit."

I should say a word yet about our youngest son, John,
who is a loving Christian . I've had to fight the fear all
these years that Satan would get him too. I've had to turn
this over to God, also.

The Scripture says that "God hath not given us the spirit of fear, but of power, and of love, and of a sound mind." I pray much for John also, as I do for all four sons. Here again I ask the Spirit's help. Romans 8:26, 27 says that the Spirit helps us in our daily problems and with our praying because we do not know how to pray as we ought.

So it is becoming more and more clear to me that I myself can do none of the things God requires, but He can do all of them in me. The more you realize this, the more you will become a mature Christian.

Another thing that helps is opening your heart to other Christians and letting them help you—by advice, by love, and by prayer with you and for you. We cannot very well do it alone.

When we received your desperate letter we thought you might want to come and live with us for a while, but after talking to you and your mother by phone it seems clear you are planning to settle there. This may be best. I am sure you can walk in the power of the Spirit there also. We pray for you daily, just as we do for our own children. We love you dearly. Write and tell us whatever is on your heart.

The Spirit will make you love everybody (not make you want to marry everybody). You will see things in a new, crystal clear way—about your boyfriend, for instance.

May God bless you as you have never been blessed before.

Love,
Ethel

12

THE LORD SUSTAINS THE WIDOWS

Faye Byers

A November Afternoon Turns to Spring

For three days, at mealtime, I fed my two-year-old son from my plate so that my husband, Cecil, wouldn't know that I was fasting. The third day, while my children were taking their afternoon naps, I glanced across my bookshelf and saw a book that had been there for six months untouched. It was a gift from a lady, who, I'm quite sure, had no idea of the teaching in the book. It had looked uninteresting and until this moment its contents were unknown to me. I picked up the book and began to read Smith Wigglesworth's personal testimony of receiving the baptism of the Holy Spirit when he was by himself. I believed that if he had received it through praise then I could too.

I knelt alone by my davenport that afternoon in November and began to visualize the work of Jesus on the cross for me. Then I began to thank Him and praise

---

Faye Byers and her late husband, Cecil, grew up in Oregon. They were in charge of the Silverton Hills Mennonite Mission for three years. In 1955 the family went to Mexico to begin the witness in which Faye is still engaged. Cecil was killed in the crash of a crop dusting plane in 1970.

Him. As I yielded my entire being to Him in praise and
thanksgiving, His reality flooded my soul. I found Him
to be truly the Rewarder of those who seek Him. I don't
know how long I remained in this ecstatic condition
praising Him in an unknown tongue. I found out that
compared to experiencing Jesus, the tongues were not
that important.

The Bible became a new book to me. My husband immediately saw the change in me. Three months later
Cecil also received a similar filling of the Spirit. The day
following my experience, while I was reading my Bible, I
felt uncomfortable because of being bothered with
hemorrhoids; then I remembered that Jesus is the same
yesterday, today, and forever. By faith I believed that He
would heal me. Without even praying about it, He
healed me. From that time to this I have been in almost
perfect health.

How easy it became to witness to the unsaved! Eagerly
Cecil and I began telling friends and relatives of our new
faith and joy in the Lord. We were not understood by
some, but this did not dampen our spirits.

I Was a Good Girl

Before my personal encounter with Jesus by the
davenport in our living room that November afternoon
fears had kept me from witnessing freely even though my
goal from the age of eleven, as I grew up in Oregon, was
to be a missionary.

Even though I memorized Scriptures, read my Bible
regularly, and won prizes in junior meeting contests, I
did not find the Word a delight and food for my soul. I
read with an attitude that I was doing God a favor and

perhaps with the idea that I was earning merits by reading it. Several times after I was in bed I got up and read the Bible because I was afraid the house might burn down if I didn't.

I knew nothing about the Holy Spirit until I attended Hesston College in Kansas for two years. There I jealously listened to some of the older girls talking freely about the Spirit of God leading in their lives. I wondered how I could ever find the Lord so real in my own life.

Within the first year after my husband and I were married, we sold our dairy cows to prepare ourselves for full-time mission work. We planned to attend Ontario Bible Institute in Canada. We hoped to study five months a year and work the remaining time during the three-year training program they offered.

Just before we were ready to leave, our home congregation, the Zion Mennonite Church near Hubbard, Oregon, asked us to superintend the mission they had opened in the Silverton Hills. We accepted the appointment and continued for three years. This in reality turned out to be our preparation for further service.

Helped Much by Evangelists

During this three-year period God spoke to us through various individuals and through several district meetings. As far as we knew, we were yielded to God and doing His will. Then I was awakened by one of George R. Brunk's shocking statements. "Many Sunday school teachers and church workers are not filled with the Spirit," he said. It was a new thought to me. Although I was not aware until then of this need in my life, I decided to answer his altar call. I didn't want to miss out if God had something more

to offer me in my Christian life. By faith I claimed the
fullness of the Spirit that night in a simple prayer.
Though my life did not seem to change in any noticeable
way, yet I made an effort to enjoy the Word and I
continued as faithfully as I knew how to perform my
duties as a mother and as a worker in the church.

When Ed Miller held meetings at our mission about a
year later, he asked, "How many here have been filled
with the Holy Spirit?" I remember that I was the last one
to raise my hand. By this time I had come to the conclusion that if I was filled with the Spirit, I would be bolder
to witness and have more power in other areas of my life.

One day after Cecil and I had given our testimonies in
a district meeting we were approached by a brother in
the church who asked us if we believed that signs and
wonders were for us today. He also asked us if we
believed that Jesus still heals today. Our answer was that
we had never given it much thought, but surely it must
be so.

We were invited to join a prayer group with several
Mennonite couples who met occasionally. But because of
the distance and because of our involvement in mission
work, we did not attend.

Awkward in the Presence of Tongues

Someone told us that those who went to that prayer
meeting spoke in tongues. We had nothing against that.
We wondered, though, if we wouldn't feel out of place.
We didn't know what we'd do while the others talked in
tongues.

Sometime later, when I saw one of the ladies of this
prayer group, I asked if it was true that she spoke in

tongues. When she admitted that she did, I asked her how she did it. She smiled and replied, "I just praised the Lord."

My hunger was whetted as I saw the joy of the Lord in her. Although I had no time to ask her further questions, I returned home telling God that if tongues are for today, I wanted them too.

The doubts were removed from my mind at a Holy Spirit meeting on the Western Mennonite School campus near Salem, Oregon, in November 1954 when several of our district ministers shared their experiences and teachings. I *knew* then that I did not have the fullness of the Spirit.

They did not mention tongues nor did they give instructions on how to be filled with the Spirit. But I was painfully aware that boldness in witnessing was lacking in my life as well as other characteristics of those that had served the Lord so freely in the Book of Acts.

I went home fully persuaded that I needed to find God in a new way. I began to seek Him with all my heart. Romans 6 was brought to life in me by the Spirit. By faith I reckoned myself to be dead to sin and alive to God.

Growing in Spite of Setbacks

About a month after Cecil received the baptism, we attended one of the prayer meetings we had been invited to earlier. For the first time we heard messages and prophecies given in tongues, along with their interpretations. The joys we received were incomparable.

At this time in our lives we were jolted loose from our complacency, where we had comfortably settled down to serve. We felt God calling us to leave the mission in

Oregon, where so many others were willing to take our places, and go to Mexico where the need was greater and where volunteers were few.

Though we were not accepted by the mission board, the reality of the Lord and His Word gave us faith to go. Friends and relatives looked on with reservations, but God clearly opened the door.

In spite of our immaturity and lack of wisdom, God blessed us with souls, prospered us with health, and provided our material needs. It has been twenty-one years ago since we came to Mexico. It has been very rewarding to see the faithfulness of the Lord in fulfilling His promises to our children and to the Mexican people.

Through His strength we were able to face many disappointments and trials as well as persecutions in the work. His strength has continued to give me grace to serve along with my children since the accident that took my husband's life in a crop dusting plane in 1970.

I've grown in understanding and in knowledge of the Word and in love for our wonderful Lord. I've learned how the fruit of the Spirit and the gifts all fit together to equip us to live a Spirit-filled life. Every day the Word becomes deeper and richer to me as I realize that there is yet much to learn and to appropriate until the day of His appearing.

Although He continues to deal with me in His mercy, no other single event has influenced the course of my life as much as the initial empowerment of the Holy Spirit. Each time that I see this experience transform the life of a Mexican Christian, it strengthens my own assurance that this power is available for each Christian today.

13

HIS SPIRIT IS A FIRE WITHIN

Ron and Bev Gibson

Ron Speaks

"His word in my heart is like fire that burns in my bones, and I can't hold it in any longer" (Jeremiah 20:9, *The Living Bible*).

In the fall of 1963, Evangelist Joe Esch held revival meetings at our church. What tremendous meetings they were! The Lord moved mightily in Brother Esch and many new Christians were won for Christ; many people also rededicated their lives to Him.

In one of those evening services, Jesus touched me. Various thoughts flashed through my mind—my sin, my selfish living, the uncertainty of life, the joy and peace our friends were experiencing, their beautiful testimonies and the reality of Jesus in their lives, and my responsibilities as a husband and father.

The evangelist encouraged us to give our whole life to

Ron and Bev Gibson live in Valparaiso, Indiana, where they own the Ron Gibson Pontiac Auto Dealership. Ron is vice president and treasurer for Heinhold Commodities in Chicago and is a church elder. Bev chaired a Christian women's organization and enjoys sewing and crafts. The Gibsons and their three sons sing together and have recorded an album.

Jesus and to allow Him to become Savior and *Lord* of our life. Then a new thought struck me. I had asked Jesus to forgive my sins and save me, but I had never allowed Him to become Lord of my life and take full control. That night after years of struggle and frustration, I asked Him to take His rightful place.

Such a wonderful peace came over me. I can't explain it, but it was real. I confirmed my decision by standing to my feet; at the same moment my wife, Bev, committed her life to Jesus in the same way. How beautiful God's timing is, to draw us closer to Him at the same moment, a husband and wife united in Jesus!

Usual and Unusual Christians

Before that evening when I made Jesus Lord in my life, I was a "going through the motions" Christian. I was twenty-seven years old, married, and father of twin sons, age four. Our marriage up to that point had been mostly happy, but we had our frustrating moments—moments of arguments, financial worry, and pressure to succeed. We lacked inward joy and peace within.

Earlier in the same year, two married couples whom we knew well experienced what they explained to us as "the Holy Spirit baptism." They were excited, happy, and joyful nearly all the time. They talked about Jesus everytime we were with them. In fact, sometimes it was downright embarrassing! They never seemed to run out of things to mention that the Lord Jesus was doing. They were able to quote Scripture after Scripture relating to the marvelous promises of God. They spoke excitedly about reading the Bible late into the night. Jesus was certainly in the center of their lives. Their excitement about

Jesus caused me to look into the Bible for answers. Obviously they had something which I didn't, and I wanted to find out what it was.

Step by Step to a Climax

The eight years following my experience at the revival meeting were a time of growth, getting to know Jesus better. Then in 1971 my desire for the Lord intensified even more. Up to that point, I was more or less satisfied with the fact that my family knew Christ, but I had no strong desire for others to find Jesus.

That year I heard a committed Christian businessman speak in a weekend retreat. He challenged us to dedicate ourselves to the task of winning souls for Jesus Christ at our places of business or wherever the Lord gave us opportunity. I dedicated my office for that purpose.

During the following months of 1971, the Book of Acts came alive for me. I read it many times, especially the verses that related how the believers came to know the Lord Jesus and how they received the Holy Spirit. My wife and I had many discussions about Holy Spirit baptism. We knew friends who had experienced this infilling, some of whom spoke in tongues. We saw the beautiful lives that resulted from this fresh anointing. The reality of Jesus shone through them. The Word of God confirmed this truth about the Holy Spirit. I wanted the fullness and power of the Spirit to be at work in my life.

Late in 1971 Luke 11:13 really spoke to me. "If you then, who are evil,know how to give good gifts to your children, how much more will the heavenly Father give the Holy Spirit to those who ask him!" All I needed to do was ask.

In bed one evening about 11:00 I asked the Lord Jesus to fill me with the Holy Spirit to enable me to witness more effectively for Him. As I lay there praying, warmth began at my feet and went up through my body as though someone were covering me with a blanket. A great feeling of peace engulfed my entire being. I was surrounded with the love of Jesus. I sensed His presence. I worshiped Him in my heart. I did not speak in an unknown language as in the Book of Acts, but I knew in my heart that Jesus had filled me with His Holy Spirit.

For the next five or six months Satan kept raising doubts in my mind on whether I had really been filled with the Holy Spirit. I kept asking the question, "Do you have to speak in unknown tongues to prove you have received the Holy Spirit?"

During the spring of 1972 our congregation was studying a series of Bible lessons in preparation for the Holy Spirit Festival to be held at Goshen college. It was a beautiful study,truly inspired by the Lord. As our weekly prayer group in church considered the biblical truths in this study, I became more convinced that Jesus had filled me with the Spirit that evening several months before.

And Tongues Too

Several days after receiving that assurance in my heart, I was driving home from my Chicago office. It was a beautiful May evening and I was thinking how wonderful God is. I began praising God in song. As I was singing, a few unknown syllables came from my mouth which I had never heard before. These syllables or words sure weren't from the English language. Each time I started to say something, these unfamiliar syllables came out. After starting three or four times, the syllables just began to flow forth as though I had been speaking this way all my life. I was deeply aware of the Lord's presence in the car with me. I continued to praise Him in this new edifying way.

As I drove home that evening, I don't remember the familiar landmarks. In fact, I don't even remember driving home! I must have prayed in this manner for twenty or thirty minutes, I can't be sure, but all of a sudden I was home in our driveway. I thought I had floated home. I shared this experience with my wife. I was so excited I wanted to tell everyone I met, but the Lord showed me in His loving way the time and place for such sharing. He didn't want me to bowl anyone over!

I certainly have not attained perfection by this experience. The Holy Spirit, the Bible tells us, gives all honor, glory, and praise to Jesus. This experience has helped me to realize the reality of Jesus. I don't believe we should limit His power and what He is able to do if we allow Him to. The Scriptures tell us that all power in heaven and earth is given to Jesus. Hallelujah! Our source of power is the living God, through Jesus Christ. He dwells in us in the presence of the Holy Spirit. Praise His wonderful name!

Bev Speaks

Eight long years! That's how my story begins. Many emotions run through my mind as I remember the eight years following the night Ron and I stood at the revival.

I'm so thankful that the Lord is patient, long-suffering, merciful, and not pushy! If I were in His place, I'd have given up on me long ago! Maybe some of you can identify with me and my struggles. Maybe for some of you your "eight years" aren't over yet. Don't despair. Just look to Jesus! He won't lead you astray. I know that's true because I experienced it.

Those eight years were filled with intellectually trying to figure out what I was hearing all around me about the "baptism of the Holy Spirit," as some phrased it. I read many books—pro and con. For about seven years I would alternately agree with what I was reading and then rebel against it wishing I had never heard of the possibility of a Holy Spirit baptism so I wouldn't have to be responsible for my reaction. Finally, I just told the Lord that I guess He'd have to make me willing.

Gradually I began to sense an inner peace regarding the legitimacy of Pentecost-type experiences in our day and age. I even became convinced that the baptism of the Holy Spirit is truly of God (and maybe even for me). I found myself breaking free from the barriers that had been holding me back.

To my surprise, I even heard myself encouraging a friend to be open to God's leading because I was convinced, after having studied and observed changed lives, that the baptism of the Holy Spirit is truly an enriching and fulfilling experience! And yet I, myself, didn't know if I could ever bring myself to ask God for this special manifestation of Himself in my own life.

At times I felt pressured by family and friends to ask for the baptism. I was convinced, however, that I was truly a child of God, even though I had not received the baptism of the Holy Spirit. I continued to tell the Lord my situation. (Guess what? He already knew!) I told Him that I was His child. I truly desired His guidance and blessing in my life. I really wanted to know His will for me. But I was frightened by the unknown. And I wasn't sure what some of my Christian friends would think. So I asked Him to be gentle and lead me step-by-step.

How I love Him for being so understanding! He knew the exact formula that would draw me closer to Him! Praise His name!

Let me share with you another need of mine which God understood and met. I was afraid that my husband, whom I love very much and who also loved the Lord, might accept the baptism of the Holy Spirit before I would. He was also much in prayer and searching about the Holy Spirit. This bothered me for two very silly reasons: (1) Ron and I were very close and shared everything and I was afraid of being left out and (2) I had seen some misunderstandings occur in marriages regarding the work of the Holy Spirit. But as I prayed about this, the Lord gave me peace.

God Prepared My Heart

During what seemed to be a lull in my seeking, we received a brochure announcing the Festival of the Holy Spirit to be held in Goshen, Indiana, in May 1972. This struck an eager and receptive spot in my heart. I anticipated the Festival with great excitement.

Perhaps I should explain my anticipation a little more at this point. I had been raised by my dear Christian parents in the Mennonite Church. At times during my teens I inwardly rebelled against the church, but now I had three sons and could see many benefits in our heritage. I also realized by this time that the Mennonites were not the only Christians. I knew there were Christians in all denominations, but I felt a strong tie with my church, and I still do.

During the times Ron and I discussed the baptism of the Holy Spirit, the question would invariably come up, But why doesn't the Mennonite Church teach us about it? At times I would become disappointed in my church for not having taught me what God was now showing me. So, when we received the brochure that our Mennonite Church was having a Holy Spirit Festival, we really did rejoice!

We were encouraged to prepare for the Festival by studying *50 Days* by Howard H. Charles. This was a genuine blessing, although at times I became discouraged and thought, "Oh, my, it's just another study." You see, I had already been through almost eight years of that. I wanted the reality.

During this time I was helping guide a Bible study for ladies. But I was so inadequate. I remember feeling like such a failure before the Lord. After one of my frustrating attempts to teach the ladies, I went home and cried to Ron, "There's got to be more—or it isn't worth it!"

Well, the Lord showed me that there is more. As we worked through the Howard Charles studies in preparation for the Holy Spirit Festival, I became convinced that the studies had been planned by God just for me.

Probably the most important lesson for me was the one titled "Filled with the Spirit." As I prepared for the Wednesday evening study and read the assigned Scripture, I responded at the conclusion of the lesson: 1. I now see that the Spirit can only control as much of my life as I am willing to turn over to Him. That is a sobering fact. 2. Today I will deliberately surrender myself as completely as I know how to the Spirit for His work in and through me for God's end in the world.

It was a beautiful vow that I made to God and He honored it.

God Increased the Pressure

That evening after church God seemed to say to me, "You wanted Me to let you know if this truly was for you from Me. Well, it is. Now is your time."

I was trembling with anticipation. Yet when a sister in the church, who sensed my need, came to me and asked if I wanted to pray with her, I declined politely. I know it was pride, but I had to settle this just between God and me! She said she would pray for me.

On the way home, I began to tremble again. I was afraid of this emotion and asked Ron to pray for me. Afterward, I sensed a quieting and the Lord's presence enfolding me. The next morning, the same feeling of urgency came upon me again, but this time I was not frightened. I just knew I had to get alone with God. I knew that today was going to be special for God and me.

Eagerly, I helped my husband off to work, assuring him I would be fine. I got the boys on their school buses. Then I reached for my devotional book. I began to worship the Lord and thank and praise Him. As I began to sing a little chorus, "Thank you, thank you, Jesus," a syllable came to my mind and I said it aloud. Then a whirlpool of warmth swirled about me as I sat praising God in a heavenly prayer language.

Truly God honors an honest searching heart in spite of all the failures and mistakes. Oh, to praise His name— what a privilege!

As the Scripture indicates, this experience has been edifying to me spiritually; it has endowed me with more of His love and power. (See 1 Corinthians 14:4.)

Now I Practice the Presence of Jesus

A few days after experiencing this added blessing in my Christian life, I was really bombarded by thoughts from the enemy. I cried and said to Ron, "What have I gotten myself into?" And then almost instantly, the Holy Spirit reminded me, "Remember, this wasn't your idea. It's God's plan for your life. He'll not fail you." Again I was so grateful for the definite experience God had given me. No longer could doubt keep hold of me for long.

The one special thing I thank God for is the new reality of Jesus in my life. Friends may criticize me, but I'll always know that this truly was God's plan for me.

I want to thank Him for a new awareness of His presence with me. Once before my baptism with the Spirit I made a New Year's resolution to practice the presence of God in my life. Now I enjoy His presence as I eat lunch, as I'm driving, while cleaning, while watching the noon news—all the time. It's great and I don't have to practice anymore.

My prayer life has become so much more vital. I have received definite answers to prayer and a peace in other areas of my life that before would have bowled me over. Of course, God's Word is still the key to a rewarding walk with Him. He continues to reveal more and more to me each day about His love for me and His will for my life.

"Shout with joy before the Lord, O earth! Obey Him gladly; come before him, singing with joy" (Psalm 100:1, 2, *The Living Bible*).

14

A THRILLING NEW CHAPTER

Mildred Heistand

A Broken Missionary Returns Home

For years I had lived in Africa. But I had worked myself out of a job. The winds of change were sweeping across that large continent. Trained nationals were taking over elementary teaching jobs at our mission schools. So I returned to the United States wondering what God might have in store for me.

But so much had changed in my absence: My home was dissolved—father had passed away during my last term on the field. My church was broken—our pastor resigned three months before I arrived back. My health was gone—doctors advised me to remain in the United States.

A new chapter in my life had begun. What could I do to settle back quickly into the American scene? Teach? Yes, perhaps. The week before school was to open there were still thirty-seven vacancies in our county that fall. I

Mildred Heistand served in Ethiopia with the Eastern Mennonite Board of Missions. On her return to the States, she taught public school at Ephrata, Pennsylvania. She spent a recent leave of absence with the Summer Institute of Linguistics at Ukarumpa, Papua, New Guinea, teaching second grade at Aiyura Primary School.

applied for a job and was given a school providing I took work to upgrade my qualifications. "Study the new math and science," they advised me. Things were working out better than I could have hoped.

Within a week I was settled in my apartment, fully furnished by friends, and given the use of a car for one year. I knew God cared about me and that He loved me, but a deep turmoil tormented my heart. What lay ahead? Why had the door to the foreign field closed so abruptly? What was happening in my beloved home church? Why had it splintered and broken? What was wrong? What could I do to mend some of the hurts? There was bitterness in my heart about some of the things that had happened. I begged off each time folks asked me to give a talk.

Living alone for the first time in my life, I became honest with God and told Him, "I can't pray. There's no use mincing words any longer." God understood, yet He loved me and made me realize how tenderly He cared about me. Little by little He led me to see I first needed to forgive my fellow Christians. Regardless of what had happened in my absence, I needed to forgive. "Love them as you never loved them before," the Lord told me. This took some effort because my family was now going to another church. "Forgive them and accept them though you don't understand," God insisted. And who was I to resist Him?

Through those long evenings of living alone I read, studied, and took up all kinds of activities to fill the void in my heart. But still I was bothered by an inner restlessness. If only I could pray as before. There must be something more. I read biographies of persons God used to do great things, but I fell far short of the pattern. What was the key?

Trusted Friends Reveal the Secret

Then a friend arrived from Africa. Something about her was different. I had known her from working with her on the field, but now she was changed. What had happened? We planned a weekend visit with another friend who had also returned recently. I listened to their stories of spiritual peace and power but feared to ask any questions lest I should be drawn into some strange ideas. Yet my heart longed for the peace and joy which radiated from their very beings.

That Sunday evening I met a couple who also had that special radiance shining from their faces. Whatever their story, however late the evening, I had to hear it.

As soon as they stepped into my friend's apartment, I was listening to a word from the New Testament about the Holy Spirit that I had never heard before! At least it seemed something I had never heard. For the first time in my life I understood Jesus to be not only the Savior but also the Baptizer in the Holy Spirit. Then someone switched on the TV set. Together we listened to Kathryn Kuhlman who continued to explain about the Holy Spirit from the very same verses in John 16 we had just read.

As she explained the Word, faith grew in my heart. At the close of the program we joined hands together. I asked God to wash away all that was not of Him, all the hurts and the troubles, and to fill my heart with His precious Holy Spirit. That moment He moved in and filled my heart with a love I'd never known before and a real desire to read and study His Word. I could not deny that I had been washed. I felt clean. The old hurts were gone. Everything had become new. What a night that was as God continued to minister to my spirit!

Life Can Be All New

The following days I was literally living in the Bible. I had no time for breakfast. People at school asked me what had happened. I taught my class with a joy and radiance unknown before. I knew God was with me. I prayed for His love to surround every child I taught. Changes were immediate in my classroom. My worry about needing to find another job vanished. At the close of the day I went home singing instead of being exhausted as before.

Three years earlier a teacher in New York had sent me the book, *Aglow with the Spirit*, by Robert C. Frost. Although I had tried to read it, I hadn't gotten very far in it before I put it back on the shelf. Now this book caught my attention again. As I read it, my closed mind opened up. The whole tongues teaching as he explained it began to make sense. I yearned for a deeper, personal, present-tense experience. I had read enough. I closed the book and said out loud, "Lord, if there is anything to what this author is saying, I need it and I need it right now." Suddenly there flowed from my tongue a new prayer language I had never learned. The presence of the living Christ flooded my apartment that night. He was right there with me.

At this point I didn't know anyone beside my few friends who had had such an experience, and they lived far away. Was there anyone else who shared this experience who lived close by? Ever so gently the Lord led me to one after another, most of whom were as new as I was. We shared and grew together in the things of the Spirit. One here and one there would share just a bit of what God was doing. One by one we came to share the same experience.

An Old Missionary Made New

Seven months later the Lord led me back to visit Africa. His first gentle urging was when he prompted someone to give me the down payment on my ticket. Then He provided a travel companion. What a joy to realize God had also met my brothers and sisters in Africa! God was doing a new thing among them, building His church and empowering them to do His work. God was suddenly doing what the missionaries had prayed He would do. We longed to see a strong church established in that land, for one by one the responsibilities were put upon younger shoulders. Now it was clear that God was in control and that He had promised to do a new thing. He would make His people a mighty power in the land, to stand against all the forces of the enemy. What a joy to continue in prayer for the African church.

These initial discoveries are but the beginning. Stepping out in faith is a way of life for me now. People may not understand, but when God urges, then I need to move out in obedience. Each move leads me on to the next commitment. The joy and the peace that accompany each new step are truly wonderful.

I believe that God has a plan bigger for each of us than we have yet seen. All He wants is for us to obey as He leads. All praise to Him!

15

MELTED, MOLDED, AND FILLED

Carolyn and Fred Augsburger

Carolyn Shares

The room became full of the light of God's presence when I was baptized with the Holy Spirit. I had not been seeking such an experience. At that time, 1960, we had not heard of Mennonites being filled with the Holy Spirit. (This was two years before Fred's baptism in the Holy Spirit.) My baptism came as the result of my honest confession of my sinful needs to God while serving Him.

That particular morning, only three of us women came to the weekly Bible study. The fact irked me. Eight other women who usually attended this prayer group were too busy to come to pray during this week of revival meetings. I criticized them. The entire congregation had been called to fasting and prayer, but only three of us took time out for conjoint prayer!

Thank God, the Holy Spirit led us to read Isaiah 58 that morning although I had come prepared to teach a

Carolyn (King) and Fred Augsburger provide pastoral leadership at the Berean Mennonite Fellowship, Youngstown, Ohio. Carolyn teaches first grade at the Youngstown Christian School. The Augsburgers have been engaged in extensive evangelistic work for fifteen years.

different Bible lesson. How God crushed me to nothingness through His Word: "Behold, in the day of your fast ye find pleasure, and exact all your labours" (v. 3). (There had been picnics and we were busy with canning and extra housecleaning.) "Ye fast for strife and debate" (v.4). (I had been very critical.) "Then shall thy light break forth as the morning . . . the glory of the Lord shall be thy reward. . . . The Lord shall answer . . . Here I am. If thou take away from the midst of thee the yoke, the putting forth of the finger, and speaking vanity . . ." (vv. 8, 9).

The Holy Spirit searched deeply into the souls of all three of us. As we honestly admitted our sins, that room became full of the light of God's glory. His presence continued to crush me to utter nothingness. Oh, the indescribable joy that swept over us as we confessed, wept, laughed, praised, and worshiped. During a lengthy period of ecstasy, Jesus built us up and filled us with His Holy Spirit. Wave after wave of glory overflowed from the abundance of His work within us.

Growth by Stages

This baptism in the Holy Spirit was not my initial salvation, nor an end as an experience in itself; I had accepted Christ as my Savior as a child. At nineteen, the necessity of taking Jesus as my Lord gripped my understanding and I accepted this aspect of His ministry to me. At twenty-five I dedicated myself for service, wherever God would direct. Eight years later, Fred's ordination and my own consecration for the mission work in Youngstown, Ohio, was another deeply emotional experience. God healed me of a serious back ailment in

1957. None of those meaningful steps with the Lord were as satisfying as my personal Pentecost in 1960.

This has opened new and ample inner resources within me to cope with life. I have a greater desire to study God's Word. It is a pleasure to teach Bible classes and do counseling. The fruit of the Spirit has increased in my life.

However, my husband and I suffered two years of despair and doubt when we were set upon by unwise "Spirit-filled" friends, who judged us negatively by their own experiences and condemned us as not being baptized in the Holy Spirit. When we doubt God's work in us, our lives become barren.

One day in desperation I begged the Lord almost like the Baal worshipers prayed on Mt. Carmel. I pleaded with Jesus to baptize me, fill me, or whatever it was, right then, if that which had happened to me in 1960 was not the baptism. He replied to me with Ecclesiastes 3:15: "That which hath been is now; and that which is to be hath already been; and God requireth that which is past." Praise God for the assurance and peace that flooded me. I also was delivered from depressive headaches about this time.

Tongues, Prophesying, and Praise

It was about eight years after my baptism before I prayed in an unknown tongue. The Holy Spirit manifested His language in a song that first time and gave me the interpretation about "songs in the night." Even though I greatly benefited by privately praying in tongues, fear of what many of our Mennonite friends and some relatives would think caused me to resist the open ministry of the charismatic gifts of the Holy Spirit. God endeavored to break my resistance with 1 Thessalonians 5:19, 20, "Quench not the Spirit. Despise not prophesyings."

But I argued with Him. "I'm willing to prophesy in English," I said. "Please, Lord, don't ask me to give a public message in an unknown tongue." God used His Word again to hammer at my rebellion. This time He replied with Ecclesiastes 11:5, "As thou knowest not what is the way of the spirit, nor how the bones do grow in the womb of her that is with child: even so thou knowest not the works of God who maketh all." My willfulness was mainly conquered by the Holy Spirit after that.

However, I still feel reluctant to speak out a message from the Holy Spirit unless the leader of the meeting has several times asked for someone to obey what the Holy Spirit is telling them to do. The few times that I have felt compelled to speak out, testimonies have followed that verified that the messages were from God for specific needs. One time the message was for a visiting Eastern Mennonite College senior, who was struggling with agnosticism. This message God spoke through me brought him to confess his struggle and to pray for help. So, although each time I have felt like a fool for Christ, God has been glorified by my obedience.

Praise, thanksgiving, faith, and obedience become vitally important in my life. Prayer is a constant relationship with God in praises and thanksgiving rather than a necessary ritual as before. The sweet communion with God through the Spirit gifts of wisdom, understanding, knowledge, and prophecy, are immeasurably wonderful. It has been exciting to see God fulfill His promises by faith—healings, miracles, our home, spiritual spouses for our children, ministries more than we could have imagined. The rest of the promises of Isaiah 58, especially verses 8-14, have become true. I have delighted myself in the Lord. Some will say that it is out of context for me, a Gentile, to claim God's promises to the Jews. But according to Galatians 3:26-29, since I'm Christ's, I'm an heir of the promises to Abraham's children.

The most important aspect of my personal Pentecostal life is that God is endeavoring to change me into His own image by His resurrection power (2 Corinthians 3:18 and Ephesians 1:19, 20). The excitement of changing from one victory and glory to another will continue until Jesus comes, if I am obedient and continue to love and praise Him. "So, whatever it takes, I will be one who lives in the fresh newness of life of those who are alive from the dead" (Philippians 3:11, *The Living Bible*).

Fred Shares

A snow-white dove floated down through a shaft of brilliant light and landed on my shoulder. It huddled up close to my ear. I can still feel its soft feathers against my face. The dove whispered into my ear, "I am the one who baptized you with the Holy Spirit."

This took place within the first ten minutes after I had gotten into bed one night about two years after my personal Pentecost. This vision came as an answer to my desperate prayer for freedom from bondage thrust upon me by some old-line Pentecostals and a couple of Mennonites who had just come into the charismatic movement. In their enthusiasm over their own experiences, they had insisted that I was not baptized with the Holy

Spirit because I had not spoken in tongues at the time He had filled my life to overflowing.

That bondage hurt my ministry as well as my own spirit. Following this vision, great peace flooded my soul. I was free again! Also, Howard Erwin and several Assembly of God brethren affirmed the genuineness of my experience with words of knowledge from the Holy Spirit.

Destined for the Ministry

Hunger for all that God has for His servants had been planted within me as a young man by the lives of my great-uncle, Andrew Shenk; my grandfather, J. M. Shenk; and later by my father-in-law, Ben B. King, and by James Bucher. The power and Christian graces within those men was beyond that possessed by average Christians.

At 17 I received a personal inner call to the ministry. A warfare arose between my flesh and spirit in which Satan threatened to kill me if I completely yielded to the Lord Jesus. But at the age of 25, I yielded myself unreservedly to God's will and service for my life. Eight years later I was ordained and consecrated by the Holy Spirit and the Ohio Mennonite Conference for city mission work in Youngstown, Ohio.

Early in my ministry, God told me He was going to use me in a healing work, unusual to the Mennonite Church. I confessed to Him my great fears about such a ministry because of the attitude of our denomination toward most of the charismatic gifts of the Spirit prior to this time (1957). The Lord said, "Obey me and I'll take care of your inabilities and fears. I will supply the power." A few healings happened in my ministry after that even though I had not yet experienced the fullness of the Holy Spirit.

My spirit kept crying out for more of the Holy Spirit's power in every aspect of my life and ministry. That was before the present-day widespread Pentecostal movement, thus few people within the Mennonite Church could give me guidance. Privately I continued searching, praying, and begging the Lord for power.

Satan kept accusing me of unworthiness until I made some restitutions for such things as a friend's bicycle which I had damaged as a young boy, a dog that I had killed, and a few more minor things.

During 1963, in the second church (Berean) which we started in Youngstown, William Nagenda from Uganda urged me to quit looking for an experience and start praising the Lord. I did just that and relaxed. I had not been looking for the gift of tongues. In fact, if anyone had tried to convince me then that I needed to speak in tongues, I would have likely backed away from the baptism of the Holy Spirit. About six years after my Pentecost, I learned through experience that speaking in tongues is a beautiful and blessed gift when it is under the direction of the Holy Spirit rather than of the flesh.

My Own Upper Room Experience

Back in September 1962, one night at a non-Pentecostal, citywide evangelistic crusade, the Lord poured out His blessed Holy Spirit upon me in an upper room prayer meeting. I felt like heaven opened up and Jesus turned a hose on me; the Spirit flowed down over me and welled up within me. I seldom cry, but that night tears flowed freely down my face as I experienced this great and blessed cleansing and empowering. After the main meeting, Evangelist Torrey Johnson turned toward me and affirmed my experience saying, "Fred, the Lord surely did a work in your life tonight!" Praise God, He had!

The Holy Spirit brought to me great love and peace, deeper insights into the Word, more enjoyment and power in prayer, deeper commitments, and a tremendous joy in serving the Lord. He took the sweat out of Christian service (Ezekiel 44:15-18).

Called to an Evangelistic Ministry

Immediately, a close conversational type of communications began between the Lord and me through His Spirit. One morning as I walked into the church auditorium, God said silently, "Fred, I'm going to use you in churchwide evangelism." My fearful reply was, "Lord, if this is You speaking, You'll have to send the invitations. I'm not going to tell anyone." I didn't even tell my wife. Within a few days calls began coming in and have continued coming throughout the years since then from all over the United States and Canada.

My first series of meetings was at the Sharon Mennonite Church, Plain City, Ohio, a few weeks after my baptism in the Spirit. God worked in unusual ways in people's lives all that week, but especially on the last Sunday. Early that morning the Lord promised me, while I was praying, that I was going to see something happen in His house that morning that I'd never seen before. As I stood in the pulpit and opened my mouth to minister the Word, the Spirit of God flowed over that congregation in a miraculous way. More than half of the congregation got down on their knees weeping, confessing hostilities and sins, and praying for each other. Testimonies and confession went on long past the regular closing time. All the glory for this belongs to Jesus and the Holy Spirit.

Soon after my baptism in the Spirit and my call to evangelism I was apprehensive about whether the Mennonite brotherhood would accept my ministry. These fears stopped gripping me when I learned that the secret of B. B. King's evangelistic ministry was the baptism in the Holy Spirit that he experienced in the early Nineteen Hundreds at West Liberty, Ohio. I also discovered that throughout the centuries many Christians have experienced personal Pentecosts. Their lives have manifested God's power and graces. Such people have made good and lasting impressions upon history.

Release of the Gifts

In the 1960s Paul M. Miller was used of God in freeing many Mennonites to allow the Holy Spirit to express the full spectrum of His gifts through them. At an Ohio conference at West Liberty, Ohio, Brother Miller taught that all of the gifts of the Spirit are to be in operation today in the body of Jesus Christ and in each congregation.

However, many of the charismatic gifts still were not evident in my own ministry until after my wife and I attended another seminar in 1969. There God gave us a prophecy that He had been preparing us for the manifestation of more of the gifts in our lives. He had been cleansing away my denominational fears. More signs and wonders begin to follow to call people to obedience to God in both deeds and words (Romans

15:18, 19). No turning back from this way of power and glory!

As I minister in churches across the nation, I see in every congregation persons who have been baptized with the Holy Spirit. I also see Mennonites who are bound by superstitions, fears, and occult practices such as pow-wowing and charming carried over from their pagan Germanic background. Oh, that people would become hungry and thirsty for God's full blessings in order to serve Him acceptably.

He will not allow any counterfeit experience to come upon you if you first come to Him in repentance asking for cleansing before you request the baptism of the Holy Spirit. Don't allow others to bind you by insisting that you have to manifest any specific gift of the Holy Spirit. If you have asked for the fullness of the Holy Spirit, have taken care of all known sins, and have been ministered to, go forth in faith praising the Lord, and serve Him faithfully. He will bless you with charismatic manifestations when, where, and how He desires.

16
JOYFUL LIBERATION
Louella and Eugene Blosser

Louella Shares

After a two-year extended furlough we returned to Japan in August of 1971. God gave us the assurance that His timing and leading were right. Our daughter was a junior at Western Mennonite High School near Salem, Oregon, and her two brothers were in colleges of their choice. We committed them all to the Lord and anticipated serving God in building His church in Japan.

Missionaries with Problems

In less than a year our eldest son married, and before another year had passed our family was scattered in three countries. Their lives and experiences were not reassuring. They faced increasingly disturbing and faith-trying experiences. We suffered sleepless nights and days of

---

Louella (Gingerich) and Eugene Blosser have served as Mennonite missionaries in Japan since 1953. Natives of Iowa, both served earlier in China under the Mennonite Board of Missions until 1951. They were married in Hong Kong in 1949. Eugene pastored the Parnell (Iowa) Mennonite Church during 1952-53. Louella is a graduate of LaJunta Mennonite School of Nursing and Goshen College. Eugene holds a degree from Goshen Biblical Seminary.

fasting and praying. The burdens seemed unbearable and the problems insurmountable. But not so to God. He had a plan and He knew the outcome. He was preparing us for what was to come.

The Lord had led us back to the States for an extended furlough in 1969 at a time when several of our children were making transitions to American life and culture. We knew the moral and spiritual fabric of their lives was being tested. After much prayer for guidance, we were confident the Lord was leading us to First Mennonite Church at Nampa, Idaho. Having been out of the country for most of the previous seventeen years we had not realized the extent to which the Spirit of God had been working among His people with dramatic evidences. Soon we were wondering, "What is this charismatic movement all about anyway?"

Gentle Introductions to the Charismatic Movement

Nampa, Idaho, proved to be a good location to observe many evidences of what was happening. At first we were cool and skeptical, especially regarding the tongues talk. That belonged to history!

Our first encounter with tongues was in a small congregation and at that time registered a very negative charge in us. Then we encountered the "Jesus People" who came to Boise to witness and testify. We attended an open-air meeting of their group. They were definitely today's youth generation in denims, long hair, guitars, and barefeet—but they all were jubilantly happy. Their Bibles were well worn from use. They praised Jesus and testified about what He was doing for them. They spoke of the work of the Holy Spirit in their lives. We were impressed with their effectiveness. The power of the Spirit was surely evident in their lives and those who found Christ through their witness.

One evening a Catholic nun, invited to speak at our church, told how she had received the Spirit and the joy, peace, and assurance that she had found. The Bible opened to her in a new way, she said.

Changes were taking place in our thinking. Some persons in our congregation had definitely experienced the fullness of the Spirit with liberation and expectant joy and love for the brethren that was unusual. They shared with us their victories and told what their friends with whom they fellowshiped were experiencing. They spoke of the Spirit as more than a mere presence in their hearts.

Ever so gradually we became interested and open to what God wanted to show us. The Lord used a brother to challenge Louella's faith one day. She asked why he thanked God for answers to prayer when obviously they were not yet answered. He replied, "God has promised to hear and answer our prayers, so I can thank Him and know that He will answer in His wisdom."

During our first year at Nampa the Fred Augsburgers were invited by the congregation for special meetings. The congregation was really blessed through the ministry of Fred and Carolyn. They also helped Gene and me to open our hearts and understanding to the work of the Holy Spirit as they shared their insights and experiences.

Then a book was introduced to us on the contemporary movement of the Spirit among the main-line churches and the new life it was bringing to the people and congregations where hearts were opened to Him.

On several occasions we were invited to charismatic

prayer meetings. Having no good reason to refuse, we attended. Instead of the expected display of emotions, we discovered a genuine love and concern for each other. We experienced new ways of offering praise and thanksgiving to the Lord—praying and singing with arms lifted. Somehow our arms were too heavy to raise above our heads. There Gene had his first experience of hearing tongues. Imagine his surprise when the interpretation given was almost a duplicate of his sermon outline for the next morning. This experience registered a rather positive charge in our hearts. However, we still felt no real need for our own involvement. But that group's concern and fervent prayer for one another, for people in the community with special needs, for churches and pastors, as well as their hearty praise and thanksgiving, indicated a degree of spiritual life and vitality we could not ignore.

Various books we were reading spoke to us of the Holy Spirit's work in the lives of many people. We sensed that He comes in power and blessing to those who are willing to open their hearts to Him. Also we became aware through all these experiences and encounters that it was not us seeking God, but God was trying to get through to us by various influences and experiences to show us what He had to offer.

About this time we attended a meeting where David Wilkerson shared his vision and told of his call to work in the slums of New York and of the power of the Spirit in that work. We accepted this as evidence that God was releasing His power through the Spirit in a new way among His people today.

But the Lord still had more preparation for us. The last Sunday evening before our departure for Japan in 1971

we worshiped with the congregation at McMinnville,
Oregon. Led by a lay brother, the meeting was one of
praise and prayer from the beginning. Our participation
and sharing on Japan were well received. At the close of
the meeting, Oscar Wideman, the pastor, invited our
family—Eugene, Louella, and Mary Lou—to come to
the front of the church and to kneel. As many of the congregation as could laid hands on us and prayed for our
service in Japan and for the leading and blessing of the
Holy Spirit in our lives. Our hearts were overwhelmed
with this expression of Christian love.

Returning to Japan, we pondered deeply all that we
had experienced. Our hunger and thirst for a fuller
reality of the Holy Spirit and His power and fruit in our
own lives had been stimulated to the saturation point.

God's Hand at Work in Japan

That autumn Gene was asked to prepare a message on
the gifts of the Spirit for our annual mission meeting.
This was a good opportunity to examine the various
theological viewpoints and to study the new movement.
He discovered that most writers,consciously or uncon-
sciously, upheld a particular theological viewpoint. This
was true both of earlier conservative writers and of the
new movement authors. Through these studies Gene was
convinced that those who were experiencing the fullness
and gifts of the Spirit were participating in something
much closer to the New Testament ideal than were
others. Their experiences appeared to be what the
apostles and New Testament writers were describing.

About this time we were going through the deep trou-
ble and burdens mentioned in the opening paragraphs.

Our sons were struggling with problems of their own. Both required individual concern and dialogue. The Lord was teaching us patience and perseverance. The burdens were crushing us and we felt alone. God used two families to minister to one son at a crucial time. The Lord sent a missionary couple to share his burden with us. Another missionary couple prayed with us for the other son and his wife. The Lord was using people at L'Abri to minister to them in their struggles. We learned that what God accomplishes when His children obey the Spirit's promptings is beyond our comprehension.

As we were experiencing these struggles, at the appropriate time a sister at Nampa, Idaho, obeyed the Spirit and sent us the praise books of Merlin Carothers. The first book, *Prison to Praise,* introduced a whole new (until then unthinkable) concept to our faith life. Yes, we could usually find something to praise God for, but to thank Him for all things in all circumstances, as Paul says, was just too much. We surely shouldn't praise the Lord for that. We were shown that this is what the early Christians did. The devil tried to convince us otherwise, but God kept patiently working with us.

God answered our prayers. As we turned our burdens over to Him He gave us peace, encouragement, and strength. Satan would put doubts in our minds. These we would confess and God in His love gave new hope. During those days of struggle our daily song became, "They that wait upon the Lord shall renew their strength."

Louella Finds the Answer

One day at home alone I was searching the Scriptures and God showed me my unbelief. He said, "If you can really believe that with Me all things are possible [Mark 9:23], trust your sons' problems to Me and let Me manage their circumstances and find solutions for their needs." He also revealed to me my proud and prejudiced attitude regarding the gift of tongues. I confessed my sins and repented. Then for the first time I was able to tell the Lord, "I'm willing to receive the gift if You are willing." I was suddenly overcome with weeping and at the same time a deep peace came over my being. Then the Lord quietly affirmed me, "It's all right. I'll give you the ability to pray in Japanese." All these years this had been so difficult for me that I avoided audible prayer whenever possible. With thankful heart my burden was lifted and He kept His promise.

Another Holy Spirit seminar was announced in Sapporo and Gene and I decided to attend—not just as observers, but to participate fully. The messages on God's love and Jesus as Lord were great! The last evening a service of ministering in the Spirit was announced. I asked Gene if perhaps we should leave now, but he replied, "Let's stay and see what the Lord may have for us." I thought he must want to request prayer for healing of his back. (He had experienced severe back problems which required traction and medication.) So I remained there with him on the front seat. Praise and prayer ascended. People were laying hands on others and praying. People were encouraged to pray in tongues. Here I discovered that my former prejudice hadn't been overcome. My pride said, "Oh, no, that prattle isn't for me." Just then the Lord rebuked me, "Who are you to criticize My gift?"

Several brethren, among them a Catholic priest, laid

hands on me and prayed—after asking our names—a prayer I'll never forget, remembering our children and our labor for Christ. He also prayed that I might be able to humble myself and yield completely to the Holy Spirit, allowing Him to pour out His power and gifts through me for His glory. I quietly confessed my stubborn pride and committed myself to Him. Suddenly my tongue was loosed in utterances which I could not understand. I felt submerged in God's great love.

Having experienced the filling of the Spirit a number of times, I can't equate the gift of tongues as necessary evidence of infilling. At the same time I know I have something different than ever before.

What happened after that? It made a great difference in my attitude toward God, prayer, and my burdens. Jesus took from me the weights and has carried them for me. The concern remains, but I know He is faithful. I stopped playing God and trying to tell God how to answer my prayers. I devote more time now to praising Him joyfully with a sincere heart. As for tongues, I use them for what I understand they were given. In my prayer life I turn over deep yearnings of my heart to the Holy Spirit, who takes them to the Father. This is a relief. My own words have never been adequate to praise Him.

There's a great difference between giving up on others and giving the burden for them over to God. With confidence and hope Gene and I are already thanking God for His management in effectively revealing His love which will call our second son to faith and a life that will glorify God.

The joy of a liberated heart to trust God enables me to

continue praising Him. This calls for obedience on my part and occasionally for specific action, along with prayer and praise. We have a great big wonderful God! As long as He gives life, I pray that I may continue on the growing edge to keep knowing Him better and praising Him more.

Eugene Shares

I was always afraid that if I opened myself to the Spirit He might ask me to do something I wouldn't like to do. I learned, however, that the Holy Spirit is a very gentle Person. He not only produces the fruit of the Spirit in the lives of His people, but He *is* the fruit in those who allow Him a place in their lives. This thrilling discovery brought me joy and assurance as I realized I had nothing to fear. As Paul says, "For you did not receive the spirit of slavery to fall back into fear, but you have received the spirit of sonship. When we cry, 'Abba! Father!' it is the Spirit himself bearing witness with our spirit that we are children of God" (Romans 8:15, 16).

My experience has been a series of steps of faith as I opened my heart to the fullness of the Spirit. One big step was at the McMinnville church, as Louella mentioned, when my thirsting heart received their generous ministry and God poured out His blessing. Another important step was the liberation I found through praise after reading Carother's books. Regarding the struggles we were having as a family, I learned that the Spirit wants to bear our burdens, but we must let Him take them. We already knew with our heads, but not with our hearts. What joy I found when I could let Him take the burdens. I began waking up mornings with a song on my lips even in the midst of overwhelming discouragements.

The next step came at the Holy Spirit seminar which Louella described earlier. The messages there spoke to my heart just as they did to her. I had gone to the seminar with a deep spiritual thirst for more of the Spirit's work in my life. Somehow the Lord impressed upon my heart that He still had much more to give.

When the invitation was given for those desiring a deeper experience to stay for a special ministry in the Spirit, I didn't want to leave. There was praying in tongues and praising the Lord in the Spirit, but nothing emotional. I prayed silently as I waited. The tongues still seemed very strange to me. As those who were laying on hands came to me, they urged me to pray expressing any syllables the Spirit might lay upon my heart. I tried to cooperate and managed several faltering phrases, none of which had any meaning to me. Among those laying on hands was a Catholic priest with whom I had studied at Ann Arbor, Michigan, thirteen years earlier. He prayed a very moving prayer that God would anoint me with His Spirit.

While I had a deep and profound joy from this experience, I felt a lack because I wasn't able to pray freely in tongues. For a time I decided maybe tongues weren't for me, but in daily prayers I continued expressing the syllables the Lord gave me. Gradually I was able to pray with considerable freedom, and my joy increased. The Lord gave affirming experiences through answers to prayer and "coincidences" that were obviously of the Lord's doing.

In my own ministry I found greater freedom and awareness of God working in me for others. One evening

I was able at a cottage meeting, rather spontaneously, to lead the group in a service of anointing and prayer for healing for the head of the home. The following week there was great rejoicing in the family as the father shared what God had done for him. His joy was of the Lord, for he was a changed man.

To me the Bible came alive in a new way. Promises and truths stood out which I had never seen before. Formerly I read the Bible rather mechanically—a chapter or a passage a day. But now I read through several chapters before I realized it. The Bible is truly a living message of the Lord which makes me aware of His living power within me.

I still get discouraged sometimes, but when this happens I know what's wrong. I've neglected the Lord and then He withdraws from me. He cannot bless a servant who is not ready to praise and glorify Him. God is practical and asks for a practical facing of facts in experience as well as in theology. Since the Lord has given me a new freedom in the use of tongues, the deep thirst that seemed so unquenchable has been satisfied.

What joy to know His love and grace are so full and free to all. Each day I open my heart to the Lord in expectancy to see what new thing He will do today. To Him be glory and praise world without end! Hallelujah!

17

THE LUMBERJACK WHO EXPERIENCED THE BAPTISM

Byron Shenk

An Astonishing Exposure

As a fourteen-year-old lad in Oregon, I found it hard to believe my dad when he told us of the preacher he had heard the previous night. But when I saw and heard the preacher myself, I found it just as incredible. I decided he had to use makeup or special oil to cause his face to be so radiant. I certainly had never heard any minister preach with such joy and authority. The absolute confidence he expressed in Jesus' ability and desire to enter into our lives was thrilling. I was deeply moved by the way he led the congregation in worship and praise of God.

This was my first exposure to Christians who emphasized the Person and work of the Holy Spirit in the Christian life. I was rather uncomfortable and felt guilty for being in such a service. These Christians were exu-

---

Byron and Elaine (Yeakley) Shenk live at Harrisonburg, Virginia, where Byron teaches in the physical education department of Eastern Mennonite College. He has also taught at Woodstock School in India and at Goshen College. Elaine grew up in Colorado. Byron was born in Oregon and worked in the tall timber as a lumberjack for several years.

berant in their worship. I remember thinking it would be too bad for us if our ministers knew dad had taken the family to such a worship service. However, this became the pattern in the life of our family for the next four years. Twice each Sunday we attended the services of our home congregation. During the week we went to other services.

I'm glad I had this exposure. However, it was not without price. When I was sixteen my parents were brought under such pressure and criticism for attending these "other" worship services that they were no longer welcomed in our home congregation. It is difficult to express the deep pain and heartache I saw my parents suffer.

Prior to my seventeenth birthday, I committed my life to Christ. With that decision I began a search for more of God than was to be found in any denomination.

I heard of joy, power, and victory in Christ from our ministers and yet saw much joylessness, powerlessness, and defeat among our people. I observed our testimony meetings were often, "It's so difficult to be a Christian. Pray for me that I will hang on until the end." Yet in the "other" congregation the testimonies were usually punctuated with praise and testimony to the supernatural power of God to save, heal, and walk victoriously. This intimate relationship with the risen Jesus was what I longed for.

From Lumberjacking to the Halls of Learning

Following graduation from high school, I worked as a logger in the Oregon timber. These were easy times. I loved my work and found fulfillment in the rigors of lumberjacking. I earned excellent wages and enjoyed hunting and fishing for recreation. I was walking with the Lord as best I knew how.

Abruptly after three years of this rewarding work I was called of God to go to college. In September 1959 I enrolled at Goshen College in Indiana. I missed the rough and rugged life of the Oregon loggers. Yet college was exciting also because I knew unmistakably that God had called me there.

The Book of the Acts in the Sixties

At college I met Elaine Yeakley (from Colorado), the wonderful girl who became my wife during the summer of my second year. Each summer we went to Oregon and I worked in the timber. One summer, through my twin brother, we joined a fellowship of believers of diverse background who had a profound influence on my life.

This weekly fellowship seemed like "The Book of Acts of the Apostles, 1963," to me. The group concentrated on serious study of the Bible, worship, praise, and ministering to others.

The members of this fellowship were leading many spiritually needy individuals to Christ. Persons in bondage to alcohol, drugs, sex, illness, and Satan were set free. Families in the group often invited strangers into their homes overnight or for as long as several weeks at a time. I mean total strangers off the highways or out of city parks. They took these persons in, sharing their possessions and Christ Jesus with them. Some of these persons came to know Jesus as Lord and Savior. There was a great emphasis in the fellowship group on making and being disciples.

Manifestations of the supernatural gifts of the Holy Spirit occurred regularly in this fellowship. These people left me feeling Jesus had been present in person a few minutes before I arrived and He would be right back. Their intimacy with Christ could not be denied. I loved the Lord and was involved in serving humanity and the church. Yet I lacked a dimension in my life these people had—a tremendous vision of world missions beginning locally and extending to other lands. Conversation centered around the body of Christ, the kingdom of God, and the return of Christ for His body. They spoke often of the Person and work of the Holy Spirit in bringing us to maturity as disciples of Christ. I became convinced there must be more available for me as a follower of Christ.

The Blessing of the Spirit Was Extracurricular

Upon graduating, I joined Goshen College's physical education faculty. I sensed God calling me not only to teach and coach, but to minister to spiritual, emotional, and physical needs as well. I began giving serious study to the work of the Holy Spirit, considering how He might enable me to minister for Christ on the campus.

I must say here, before sharing the rest of my story, that in all my walk with God I have never had an ecstatic experience to confirm or convince me of some truth. Everything the Lord has given me has been received by raw, dry, unemotional faith. Thank God, I have enjoyed ecstatic experiences but they have always come as unexpected expressions of God's mercy or grace in the course of my daily walk, but never when I was seeking for an experience.

The answer I was seeking came to me one evening as I was reading Luke 11. We are all familiar with the Lord's Prayer in verses 2-4. In verses 5-8, Jesus gives the illustration of one who goes to the home of a friend at midnight to ask for three loaves of bread for friends who have arrived unexpectedly. Jesus concludes this account with the words, "Because of his importunity he will rise and give him whatever he needs." As I read the ninth verse, "Ask, and it will be given you; seek, and you will find; knock, and it will be opened to you," I sensed the Holy Spirit was about to teach me something important. With careful attention, I moved on to verses 10-12. "If a son asks his father for bread, fish, or an egg," Jesus asks, "will his father give him a stone, a serpent, or a scorpion?"

Jesus ends this section of teaching with verse 13, "If you then, who are evil, know how to give good gifts to your children, how much more will the heavenly Father give the Holy Spirit to those who ask him!" The Holy Spirit spoke gently, illuminating my heart and mind. I saw the entire passage dealing with my coming to the Father for food for the spiritual man. (Jesus said, "I am the bread of life" in John 6:35, and "I have food to eat of which you do not know" in John 4:32.)

It was clear to my heart and understanding that if I asked God my Father to give me the Holy Spirit (daily bread) He would do so. I became bold as I saw verses 5-13 as a promise to me.

I prayed, "Father, Your Word says You will give the Holy Spirit to those who ask. Upon that promise, I right now ask You to give the Holy Spirit to me. Father, Your Word says that if I ask I will receive. Therefore, as I have

asked, You have given to me, and I receive Him now.
Thank You for giving the Holy Spirit to me."

That was it! No feelings. No emotion. I had acted in
simple faith and obedience to the Scripture and I
believed I had received Him. I knew I had received Him.
I had a new faith to believe.

My New Anointing Expanded My Ministry

I began to grow in awareness of His presence and
power. Soon more students were coming to share their
needs and problems with me and to talk about Christ.
What a joy to be His and share Him. I found it natural to
believe that every need expressed could and would be
met by the Lord. Occasionally the Holy Spirit would
grant a word of knowledge which would enable the
person to comprehend his situation better, or help me
minister to the need more effectively. At times I became
aware of active resistance from Satan as he attempted to
keep a person in bondage. When this was revealed to me
by the Holy Spirit, I could then in the name of Jesus,
through faith in that name, challenge the evil one for his
deliverance or healing (Acts 3:16). The power of God was
released through me for physical healing by prayer. I became more aware of the presence and power of Christ in
my ministry.

Tongues Worried Me, Then Blessed Me

I struggled for five years in one area. I wanted to be an
example of one who had the Holy Spirit without speaking in tongues. This was a plague to me. I was reacting to
excess or unwise exercise of tongues. I had been turned
off by those who believed speaking in tongues was a

necessary proof of being filled with the Holy Spirit. I fought against every evidence of tongues and found faults in those who exercised tongues. I felt my prayer life was of such maturity that I did not need tongues. I see now that I was guilty of pride.

Often in prayer I came to a point where I could no longer pray. I had said it all and there was no additional word from the Lord. Yet I would have a deep burden and I found myself saying, "If only I could intercede and pray more effectively."

In 1970 I came to see that God sometimes gives messages of truth, guidance, and praise through a tongue in a known foreign language, not previously learned by the one speaking, then interpreted by another who knows that foreign language. This experience was given to personal friends of mine and I heard the similar testimony of another Christian. Likewise there were evidences of persons speaking in an unknown tongue which was interpreted (not a known language, but a message of "thus saith the Lord"), which proved to be true and strengthening to the local body of believers.

And so I was forced to recognize tongues as a gift of the Holy Spirit ("when kept in its proper place," I was quick to add). I began to say, "If God wants to give me the gift, I'll take it." But deep within me, I hoped He would never do it to me. One evening while reading 1 Corinthians 12 and 14 and related passages, the Holy Spirit said to me, "If God gives you a gift, is it good?"

"Yes," I replied. "Why?"

"Because it is from God."

"Would tongues be a good gift from the Father?"

"Yes, tongues would be a good gift."

I was shown that I believed tongues to be the least of all the gifts of the Holy Spirit. I was willing to receive the best or greatest but not one so controversial and so criticized. What spiritual pride! Again I asked God for forgiveness and cleansing.

It was another year yet before I exercised this prayer language. I had two fears to overcome: "What if Satan tricked me and I actually cursed God in tongues?" and "What if the Spirit caused me to burst out in tongues in public meetings?" As I studied Scriptures, I came to understand two things. First, there is a threefold ministry of this gift: (1) to speak to God and worship the Father, (2) to intercede for others, and (3) to be built up in one's own faith. I became convinced that the Holy Spirit does not overpower a person and cause one to speak out against his own will. From that time on, I desired this enablement.

I am thankful to report that my wife and I have a one-ness in this area due to the work of the Holy Spirit on our behalf.

Because of the gentle nature of the work of the Holy Spirit in the lives of our "full gospel" friends and of my own encounter, my wife came to a point in her walk with God where she also understood the validity of this for Christians today. Elaine says that if I had tried to force my encounter upon her she would have rejected not only my encounter, but probably the future blessing in this area she was to receive. Thank God I never did tell my wife, "I've found what you need." Only little by little did I share with her, and this was often in the presence of a small group or a friend. I did not have to drag her along to anything. The Lord led her in His own way.

I put my faith into operation late one night. I reviewed the subject of tongues once more. The gift is of the Holy Spirit. It has a threefold ministry in its operation. Acts 2:4 gave me the clue on how I was to receive this gift: "And they . . . began to speak in other tongues, as the Spirit gave them utterance." I had been waiting for the Spirit to overpower me and to cause uncontrollable babbling to come forth. I checked the Greek meaning of this verse and saw that I had to exercise my vocal cords and lips as the Holy Spirit gave the utterance. That was what I needed to know. I prayed, "Father, by faith in Your Word, I'm going to speak as Your Spirit gives the utterance. I pledge to You that every sound coming from my vocal apparatus will be to glorify God the Father, to bring others into Your kingdom, and to strengthen my faith that I might better glorify You. In Jesus' name. Amen." With that I rested a few moments in praise and worship and simply began to verbalize the speech in my mind.

My first thoughts were, "What odd sounding speech." But for forty-five minutes an endless flow of unintelligible words came forth. I never felt ecstatic or excited, but simply was empowered by His presence. A deep peace and witness from the Holy Spirit came over me. I did not believe then (or now) that I was anyone special or favored among men.

The very next day, within a period of three hours, two athletes came to talk about nagging injuries that plagued them. By the time each had gone from my office, he had not only confessed a need for spiritual healing but had prayed confessing that need to God. The Holy Spirit then witnessed to me that these were two for whom intercession was being made in my prayer language the previous night. I have experienced the same thing since.

On occasion, while praying with my prayer language, a spirit of weeping or joy will come upon me and the wonderful presence and touch of Jesus becomes real. Never have I had ecstatic feelings or uncontrollable desires to burst out in public (though I believe there may be proper exercise in public of this gift).

The prayer language has not been an end in itself for me. I am very human. I fail and act unlike Christ at times. But speaking in tongues has been a door to step through in my walk with Christ. I find my prayer more effective, my faith has increased, and I experience greater depth in praise and worship of the Father. I accept tongues as a tool the Holy Spirit grants to equip the believer. It does not make me anything special. It has caused me to be more vulnerable and I have become weaker in my own strength. I thank the Lord for providing this gift to me. My prayer and heart desire is Philippians 3:10-12. Thanks be to God.

18

MISSIONARIES WHO NEEDED TO BE BROKEN

Catharine Leatherman

Two Kinds of Deliverance

The Teen Challenge team was praising God for deliverance from alcoholism and drug addiction and for a new life within. I had a chance to give my testimony only after the meeting was over, as I shook hands at the door with the group's leader.

"I appreciated the testimonies of these young men," I said, "but I think the Lord did an even more wonderful miracle for me. He found me in a hard, shining shell of being 'good' in myself and critical of others. He broke through and I saw I was really poor and needy. To me this is an even greater miracle than that which the young men testified to tonight, who knew they were sinners."

The man's eyes lit up, and he said simply, "You know, I think you're right!"

Catharine Leatherman and her husband, John, went to Tanganyika, East Africa, as missionaries in 1936. Catharine led women's Bible classes and John taught a whole generation of black Mennonite church leaders in the Bible school and seminary. The Leathermans retired to Mt. Joy, Pennsylvania, in 1965 after nearly thirty years in Africa. John died of cancer in 1969.

Joining the Glorious Missionary Band

I was only twenty-one and John was twenty-six the memorable night our ship pulled out of New York harbor. A host of friends and well-wishers were there to see us off as we went to join the small group of eight missionaries already in Tanganyika, East Africa. John had been ordained to the ministry at Doylestown, Pennsylvania. He loved his Greek New Testament, and tried to get at the fullest meaning of the words of his well-worn Bible. Theology was meat and drink to him, and the exhortation in Jude 3 to contend earnestly for the faith once delivered to the saints found a ready response.

I had just finished college. The degree and the certificate to teach reassured me. I failed to foresee that degrees and certificates couldn't mean less to folk who, while they could not read books, could read people very well. When we had taken the doctrinal examination which our mission board required, it was gratifying to us to each receive the grade of A plus.

I felt secure about our marriage and was confident that it would be both a happy one and solid enough to survive the storm of life.

We felt that our love for each other, and our understanding and ability, was great enough for whatever might come. Like Moses at a crucial point in his life, we had decided to cast our lot with our people. We were committed to the Lord's service and we wanted our lives to count for Him.

Crushing Futility

During the next seven years on the mission field, the Lord took us in hand and taught us some lessons we needed to learn. After some language study we were asked to open a school to train African leaders and teachers. Half a dozen or so families came for this training. There were problems, of course. I'm not sure what the students learned, but I know that the teachers learned they were not as effective as they had hoped. Patience, humility, and loving understanding seemed to count for more than knowledge and supposed ability.

During these years our four children were born, and duties multiplied.

The goal of our being in Africa was to win souls to Christ. After a time there were twelve members in the little church at Bukiroba. We looked forward to the number increasing. However, our little church soon began to fall apart. One member after another was proved to be living in sin; finally there wasn't a single African Christian left in our local church. It was devastating to us missionaries. But the thing that sent us to our knees was the dismaying thought, "How is it we had so little spiritual discernment that we could think these people were right with God, when in fact they were not!" We prayed for discernment for ourselves and we prayed for revival for the African church. We got up early in the morning to have prayer meetings.

Creeping Censoriousness

Along with the feeling of being ineffective and undiscerning in spiritual matters, there was also a rising lack of concern and love within us. We carried increasing resentments and critical judgments toward others. John and I both became quite expert at being able to put blame where it belonged. The Africans were at fault because

they were demanding and not grateful. Our missionary co-workers were at fault for not being as thoughtful as they should have been. Our children were at fault for being too boisterous and noisy. (At least that was how I excused my lack of patience with them.)

We had many guests in our home, since we lived at the central station. We tried to be genial hosts, but after they had gone we would often speak critically of them.

As you can imagine, this habit of being critical of everyone else and blaming them for everything that didn't go right began to corrode our home relationship. This marriage which I was so sure could withstand all the storms of life, because our love was so deep and strong, slowly began to be less happy. On my side I felt it was because John now cared mainly for himself. I'm sure he felt the same toward me, and indeed he was right, although at the time I didn't see it. I thought of myself as a virtuous wife and mother, suffering because I was not appreciated.

During this time something happened in which I felt I must forgive a certain wrong. I said, "Yes, I forgive," and I really tried to forgive. But when I would get to thinking about the wrong I had suffered, it still rankled in my heart. I tried and tried to forgive, and I prayed God to put forgiveness into my heart. Finally I just told the Lord I choose to forgive, and I want to forgive, and I let it rest at that.

I began telling myself that I felt like an old woman. (I guess I thought an old woman feels tired and like a "has-been.") The joy and zest had gone out of living. Our first furlough to our homeland was canceled because of the difficulty of travel during wartime. It became easy for us to say, "Yes, we really feel the need to get away. We've been giving out so long, we're running dry." Well, the dryness was true, and it was plausible to explain that the delayed furlough was the reason. However, the implication was that the living waters were flowing back in America, and to find them we needed first to return to our homeland.

The Beginnings of Renewal

In August 1942 we went to Shirati hospital to await the birth of our fourth child. We were distressed that the church there wasn't able to have communion services because of disunity between nationals and missionaries. The controversy was mainly over policy concerning what money from America should be used for. So that Sunday we had just preaching, and afterward we knelt on the earthen floor of the church building beside the backless benches of mud brick. Then a spirit of penitence came down over the whole congregation. People began confessing their sins and weeping. More and more joined in until it seemed the large congregation was all groaning and crying and confessing sin to God. Never in all my life have I seen anything like it. At first I was frightened, then reassured, and finally very happy that God had heard our prayers. This revival at Shirati went on for a long time, but it was mainly among the African brothers and sisters.

In May 1943, John and I had a month-long leave from duties and decided to go to Dar es Salaam on the seacoast. Kind friends offered to keep our nine-month-old baby. We went with the three older children by lake steamer and wood-burning train the 800 or so miles to the ocean. It was a restful vacation. Then came the time to return to our home and work. Little did I realize that those few days of our return journey would hold within them the watershed of my life. In looking back I marvel how God has every circumstance under His control so that what seemed just to happen was the exact working out of His plan.

Absolute Desperation

Upon reaching Mwanza, the port of Lake Victoria where we planned to board the lake steamer for Musoma, we found that the ship would not arrive yet for a few days. We went to the Africa Inland Mission station where they kindly took us in. "Now we can have prayer meetings together," they said with a note of anticipation.

So we had prayer meetings. But such meetings! When they prayed they talked to God. I could just feel it. When I prayed, I tried to talk to God, too, but I tried too hard to phrase a nice prayer so that they would consider me a fine spiritual missionary.

After I had finished my prayer, I felt irked. My prayer was stilted and somewhat artificial, and I was sure they had noticed it.

And the things they talked about! They couldn't seem to say enough about the wonderful life of freedom and deliverance in Jesus Christ they experienced when they began literally obeying Romans 6:11 which says, "Reckon . . . yourselves to be dead indeed unto sin, but alive unto God through Jesus Christ our Lord."

It didn't take me many hours to build up a tremendous resolve. I had to know the secret of the overflowing life of these people. I recognized it as the inner experience with

God I had been yearning for for years. I said to myself, "I don't care what it costs. I must have this life!"

So I, who practically never asked anybody for spiritual help, went to a sister and told her my great longing and inquired how to get life like this. She told me she could only explain how the Lord had dealt with her. In her own desperation, she had asked the Lord to show her how she appeared in His eyes. This He did, showing her how needy she really was. Then she confessed her sins, joined herself to Jesus, and God had done the rest.

Laying Bare the Depths

When she was finished, I knew the Lord and I had to talk things out between us. I asked John to look after the children for the afternoon, took my Bible, and went into the empty mission church next door.

I knew that the Lord speaks through the Word, so I leafed this way and that in my Bible, crying out to God for His help. I asked that He would speak to me, telling me what I lacked, and what I must yet do. I wept. I even prayed for an angel to tell me what to do, so great was my hunger and longing, and so great my despair. As I wept and read, some verses began to stand out.

"Wherefore laying aside all malice, and all guile, and hypocrisies, and envies, and all evil speakings, as newborn babes, desire the sincere milk of the word, that ye may grow thereby" (1 Peter 2:1, 2). Then I saw it! The malice, the guile, the hypocrisy, the envy, and the evil speakings—all described me! I remembered how I spoke evil of our guests after their departure. I remembered how I prayed fine oratorical prayers to impress others. I remembered the guile, saying things so innocently, while trying to pull strings to manipulate people to do what I wanted.

I read the verses about wives honoring their husbands (1 Peter 3:1-6), and I realized that what I had really wanted was for John to be some kind of a super-servant who would do whatever I wished. I saw that my attitude was one of self-righteousness—filthy rags. I saw that there was a great mountain of selfishness within me wanting my own way, wanting people to think I was somebody good, wanting to build up myself even if it meant trampling on someone else.

It was devastating! I felt as if the Lord had slain me. But oh, the mercy of it. In those two hours of breaking down my false self-confidence, the dear Lord showed me my sin and delivered me from it. Since no angel spoke to reassure me, finally in "cold faith," without any warmth of emotion, I covenanted with God that from now on it would not be I any longer who directed my life, but that Jesus would be in control. I would reckon myself joined to Him, dead to sin and alive to God because of being joined to Him.

I knew I had done business with God, but I felt no burst of happiness or joy or freedom. The joy came three days later. After we arrived home, I realized that I was happier than I had ever been in my life before. And, indeed, the joy has continued to this present day.

I had never heard of the baptism of the Spirit as something that actually happens to a person, and I had never heard of the gifts of the Spirit as something one can receive. If I had heard, at least it did not register with me. But the mercy of God reached me even in my ignorance.

Neither Theology nor the Church

John had been having his own agony of soul for an even longer time than I did. During the following week he also experienced the infilling of the Spirit. To him the theology of faith was very important. Growing in grace was the big thing after the new birth. Only he couldn't seem to grow enough. Also the church loomed larger in his life than Jesus Christ. In his later testimony he would sometimes say, "I was high and dry. Very high, and very dry."

His deliverance came early one morning after he rolled and tossed his way through a sleepless night in anguish of spirit. By morning he was a new man—new because he had consciously joined himself to the Lord Jesus through the Spirit. Peace came on John's troubled waters, and new life flowed through him.

Here is an excerpt from a letter he wrote at that time:

"Dear Ones in the Lord,

"How I praise God for the great victory of His Son on Calvary. . . . What a reproach it is to me that for years I have known so little of the meaning of that death. It was only recently through the grace of the Lord Himself that I came to an actual appropriation of His death to my life as taught in Romans 6:6 and similar passages.

"To many who read these lines, this may seem strange coming from a missionary, but missionary or no, my testimony as to what the Lord has done for me must go forth without any attempt to make it appear that this is something I have always had since becoming a Christian or something to which I have gradually grown into.

"To me it has meant a crisis. The revelation to my soul

by the Spirit that 'our old man was crucified with Him' was the result of a deep and long-felt conviction of inner need on my part which was especially apparent in my general lack of the much and permanent fruit of which the Lord speaks.

"The passages that deal with the believer's dying with Jesus I had always assumed I understood, thinking that this death was some indefinable condition of sanctity to which a person gradually approaches over a number of years. I did not understand they were to be appropriated by faith just as they stood, and when that appropriation is made the Holy Spirit immediately works the reality.

"While the Lord has done wonderful things for me in the past years, still I could not be honest and say that I was gradually becoming more 'sanctified.' Now I see that in this portion of death with Jesus, it is no longer our striving and groaning to be holy and trying to appear to others what we know in our hearts we are not, but it is His glorious self within the new man, no longer I but Christ, now raised up together with Him and made to sit together with Him in heavenly places. . . . Yours in Him, John E. Leatherman."

Forgiveness, Fellowship, and Love

One unexpected result of the new life in my soul was that in the midst of my joy, and without interrupting it at all, I would suddenly remember something that I knew I must make right. I recalled a book report I had written without reading the book. So I wrote to the teacher, acknowledging what I had done, and asking forgiveness. For two months I kept remembering other previous sins, and un-Christlike attitudes, and kept asking forgiveness of the ones I'd wronged. Finally after two months the Holy Spirit seemed to get to the bottom of the barrel, and past debts seemed all taken care of.

Our home relationship improved wonderfully. As we prayed together, shared the sweetness we found in the Word of God with each other, rejoiced in the Lord together, stood together against the enemy of our souls, we found new love and tenderness and caring. The Lord helped us to be honest and to humble ourselves, asking forgiveness when wrong words or attitudes came between us. We shared the deep things of the Spirit between us within our marriage, and with our co-workers, and with our African brothers and sisters. We had fellowship such as we had not known was possible. The love just flowed out.

The Secret: Walking in the Light

The Lord kept on teaching us and illuminating our lives. God has also been working in revival in Uganda. Some of our co-workers went there on a visit and came back with the message God had given the believers there.

"If we walk in the light, as he is in the light, we have fellowship one with another, and the blood of Jesus Christ his Son cleanseth us from all sin," 1 John 1:7 declares. The Ugandan Christians said walking in the light means walking in honesty and openness with one's brethren, letting them see us as we really are before God, repenting of all that He shows us that is wrong. As we do this, the blood of Jesus keeps on cleansing, and we have fellowship together. And indeed, we found their insights to be true. This way of honesty and openness with brothers and sisters, of repenting openly before each other of all that is of darkness, does indeed result in deep fellowship with each other.

In the years that followed, fellowship groups of believers met frequently—sometimes daily, sometimes several times a week—to share the Word and to open their hearts to each other.

One African brother told us, "When we sit around the fire in the evening, we don't part before someone begins telling what God has done for Pastor Leatherman."

Thirty-four years have passed since the Holy Spirit did His special work in my life. Since then many things happened, some pleasant, some very difficult, but always Jesus has been real and His love continues flowing out. The Bible has remained a living book for me, illuminated by the Spirit. Fellowship with brothers and sisters in Jesus during these decades has been wonderfully sweet.

The message of being joined to Jesus has sometimes been met with resistance and even hostility. But it has met with acceptance in others who leave their deep heart hunger and self-despair behind and experience joy by faith in the living Jesus.

19

GOD FILLED A FARM COUPLE IN ILLINOIS

Ron Eigsti

The Festival of the Holy Spirit Was the Key

The warm, balmy June morning seemed quite normal to those attending our church that Sunday to worship God. All the worshipers filed to their classes for Sunday school as usual, but something was different in my life that morning. As I began to teach the lesson, I strongly sensed the presence of God in the classroom. I felt like I would burst with joy! Someone asked me to share the experiences of our weekend at the Festival of the Holy Spirit held in Goshen, Indiana, during June 1972.

I really don't remember what I said. The best way to put it into words would be to write "PRAISE THE LORD" in large letters across the blackboard. I do recall that the Word became alive and Jesus seemed so real, so very real, that I just wanted to praise and worship Him as Lord and King. I got more out of that lesson that Sunday morning than any one of my class members.

I wasn't always that way! For many years living the Christian life was a real struggle for me.

Ron and Elsie Eigsti have managed a grain farm at Morton, Illinois, since 1955. They are both active in the Morton Mennonite Church and served on the Illinois Renewal Committee in 1976.

Saved, but Routine

I was born again as a young teenager. I still remember how the peace that only God can give came into my life. I received the inner assurance that Jesus had taken all my sins away. Everything went fine for a while until I put my eyes on man rather than on Jesus. This resulted in my attending church regularly and going through the motions of being religious, but I didn't experience much growth in my spiritual life. Maybe it was the lack of kids my age in our church to fellowship with, but mostly I just wanted to do things my way.

As I grew physically, I did what most normal boys do—I began to date girls, one in particular. I believe now God had her picked out for me, although my conception of God's will then was that He would go along with any girl that suited my will. As I look back on it now, I can see how God overruled my self-will and brought us together according to His purpose. It is hard to put into words what one feels inside when God is pulling one way and self is pulling the other. There were things He wanted to change in my life, but I didn't have the desire to change.

Shortly after Elsie and I were married, I entered into two years of I-W service as a conscientious objector who declined to serve in the military because of my conscience against war. Through friends on this assignment, I began to see that something wasn't what it should have been in my life. Elsie was just a young Christian. I realize now that I really didn't give her strong spiritual leadership. But God was patient with us. Deep down inside I longed for a closer walk with Him, but self also clamored for expression. I was one of those of whom

Jesus said, "The spirit is willing but the flesh is weak."
But God works with us where we are and He was able to
use what I yielded to Him. I witnessed to people on the
job at the hospital where I worked.

We returned to Illinois in 1962 after I finished my period of service. By then we had the first of the three sons
God has so graciously entrusted to us. We settled down
on a farm content to be among "the quiet in the land."
But there was one problem. The desire of my inner heart
was still there. I really couldn't put my finger on what it
was. I didn't realize at that time that what was bothering
me was spiritual unrest.

I listened to a lot of radio preachers. When a Pentecostal came on, I either turned the radio off quickly or
tuned in another station. But I was eager to learn more
about God's Word. I enjoyed hearing testimonies of
people who were living dynamic Christian lives. This
really blessed me because I was shy around strangers and
had difficulty sharing my faith with people. When I was
younger and had to get up with the rest of our Sunday
school class to give a program, I always found some tall
person to stand behind. I don't know if I didn't want to
see the audience or if I didn't want the audience to see
me. I think now that it was a problem with my pride as
much as anything. I worried about what others would
think if I made a stand for Jesus.

When visiting evangelists gave an invitation at the end
of their sermon, I often felt I should go forward and rededicate my life. I guess I thought going forward would
give me more courage and that my Christian life would
be more effective.

I knew that God had more for me than I was

experiencing, so I kept searching. The devil would come to me and say, "God can't use you; you aren't even saved." He would bring doubts and times of spiritual lows. I would wrestle with these thoughts and doubts for days at a time.

The more I read and studied the Word, the more I desired to be used of God for His glory. But it also seemed to me that the more I read the Word the more Satan disturbed my thoughts and my assurance of salvation. God's Word is complete, but I wasn't using it with the power and authority that He makes available to believers.

I began to teach a Sunday school class, and the Lord began to bless and give an increase in attendance. When Elsie and I attended a conference on evangelism, we experienced fresh inspiration of the Holy Spirit which gave us new zeal to go out in the community and witness. After a few months, however, I slipped back into my old rut. We would share our blessings together and Elsie would encourage me and remind me of the good things God was doing in our lives. We praise the Lord for that, but still things weren't happening the way we read about in Acts or in our own Anabaptist history.

A New Dimension of Joy

About this time we heard a Festival of the Holy Spirit was to be held in Goshen, Indiana, in June of 1972. We were part of a group in our church who had been meeting once a week for Bible study and prayer. We were searching the Scriptures for answers about healing, fasting, gifts of the Spirit, and something called "speaking in tongues." Many books on these subjects could have helped us, but it seems we were led to look directly into God's Word. I look back on this now and can really praise God for it.

God worked things out perfectly so Elsie and I could go to Goshen. We arrived on the campus where the Festival was held just in time for the first service. We were good Midwestern Mennonites (don't ask me to define those terms!). Now try to imagine what went through our minds when we saw all those people raising their hands and praising the Lord together. It was an astonishing experience, women in little white coverings and men in plain coats raising their hands and saying things like, "Praise the Lord" and "Hallelujah," out loud. What a shocker! We didn't feel uncomfortable, however, because we could sense the presence of God there. We had read in the Bible about raising holy hands and giving praise to God.

At those meetings we saw people healed and other things happening that are recorded in the Book of Acts. We also witnessed our Mennonite brothers and sisters receiving the baptism with the Holy Spirit. Some even spoke in tongues as the early Christians did on the day of Pentecost. I had heard that some people did these things, but as far as I was concerned such activities were reserved for emotional Pentecostals. I knew such evidences of the work of the Spirit are mentioned in the Scriptures but I didn't think they were for today.

The meetings were a real blessing to us: we could feel God's presence, especially in the evening sessions when praise was offered to the Lord. I found it rather easy to lift my hands at least half way. (I didn't want to get carried away with anything.)

I had more questions than answers in my mind as we were driving back to Illinois. What is this baptism "with" or "in" the Holy Spirit? Do I have it? If I were to get it, would I speak in tongues? The things that happened just weren't according to the way I had the Holy Spirit programmed.

The first thing I did back in Illinois was to read the Book of Acts again. "If God did it then, why can't He do it today?" I asked myself. We returned home on a Monday. Tuesday was the night for our Bible study. Everyone was eager to hear about the Festival. Our pastor had also attended and he reported on the things he had experienced. After the sharing period someone said, "Let's pray for this to happen here and now!" And that's what we did.

I really don't know how it started, but God began to pour out His Spirit in a tremendous way. Everyone began weeping, confessing sins, praying to be used more of God, and asking to be filled with the Holy Spirit. There was a time of brokenness before God. All had hands laid on them for the filling of the Holy Spirit and this was followed by a time of rejoicing and praise. No one spoke in tongues that evening, but almost all have experienced a prayer language in the Spirit since that time. This meeting really changed the lives of the ones who were there.

It was after midnight when I got home. Elsie had stayed home with the boys because of the long weekend away from home. Good news loses something when you wake a person from a sound sleep around 12:30 a.m. She was glad to hear about it, but it didn't really soak in until we went through it again the next day.

The Personal Dimension Is Important Too

A day later I realized honestly before God that I had enjoyed His presence around me but I still hadn't opened up and let Jesus fill me, mostly because of some hang-ups I continued to have. While everyone was enjoying the Lord, I was still analyzing and trying to fit the Spirit into one of my pigeonholes. I told God I was already filled with the Spirit and I would accept something like the gift of healing or miracles.

I began to make a more thorough search in the Word, knowing already what it said but hoping God had changed His mind. But there it was, "Jesus Christ the same yesterday, and today and forever" (Hebrews 13:8). The Lord spoke and said, "Ron, the problem is with you." Sometimes we know in our hearts we are wrong but our pride keeps us from admitting it. All God was doing was answering my prayers and the deep longing of my heart for more of Him. But I wanted God on my terms, not His.

The most difficult part of this whole thing was to call a brother and make some things right. Humility doesn't come easy for me, but it's the way of the cross. I called him and told him I had to see him at once. It didn't make any difference that we both had plans that night, our business would only take a minute. When we met I said, "Let's cut out the small talk and get down to business. I was wrong about everything I said about the baptism in the Holy Spirit. I want to ask your forgiveness for anything I might have said to offend you. Now pray for me."

He was rather shocked and said he'd never prayed for anything like that before because he was just new in this spiritual experience himself. Well, he did pray for me. I waited, and waited, and nothing happened. I was waiting for an "experience" and failed to see the Baptizer, Jesus. When I left that brother's place that evening, I did have a sweet peace and the assurance of faith that God had done something.

Several days went by and I began praying and seeking the Lord again. I had heard of some of the experiences of other people and I thought unless it happened to me the same way, it wasn't real. I recall vividly going to bed one night soon after the visit with my brother in the Lord and asking God for His will and way in my life. I made an unconditional surrender of my life.

I was awakened about 5:00 a.m. with a start. It was as if I heard something unusual. I got up, dressed, and went to the kitchen. I thought as long as I was up, I might as well eat and get an early start for the day. I picked up my Bible and began to read in Colossians. I started at chapter one and observed how Paul described the Lord Jesus to the Colossians. I began to think how wonderful it was to know Him. Then my thoughts of Jesus turned to prayer and the next thing I knew I was thanking and praising the Lord Jesus Christ. Soon the room was filled with the glory of the Lord. God was there, Jesus was there, the Holy Spirit was there, and that was about all I could take. I felt like a bottle of soda that had just been shaken and then opened. Praise tried to come out that only could be uttered by the Spirit to the Father. I couldn't think of anything else to say to God so I just opened my mouth and He filled it. Hallelujah!

When I opened my eyes sometime later, I fully expected to see Jesus, but everything was the same, except myself. Praise God!

Sharing Must Be Discreet

This might seem to be the end of the story, but for me it was only the beginning. It was like opening a new door to my spiritual life. Sometimes when God blesses us, it seems to wear off after a while. But this has been a lasting, growing experience. As I studied for the Sunday school class that morning, God's Word took on a new dimension. I saw things I had never seen before. I could hardly wait to get to church! But I soon found that not everyone was looking for the dimension of spiritual life that I had found. I learned quickly what things I shouldn't say and many times not to say anything at all.

As I share these things, I am aware that I'm opening myself to criticism, but maybe my testimony will help someone who is experiencing the same struggles I did. God works differently in each life. He gives us what we need, not always what we want. He worked much differently and moved more quietly in Elsie's life, but He did work and is still working.

When sharing with different people, I don't expect them to have the same experience I had; I only want them to see the same person, Jesus the Baptizer in the Holy Spirit. Only Jesus can equip us and anoint us with power to do His work in this world. I have found the quality of life that Paul describes as "righteousness, and peace, and joy in the Holy Ghost" (Romans 14:17). All glory to Him!

20

FROM OLD ORDER AMISH TO NEW PENTECOSTALISM

Harvey Graber

Stimulated by Circumstances

Personal friends told my wife, Miriam, and I of God's visitation to the Mennonites at a winter Bible school in Loman, Minnesota, in 1954. When we first heard that unusual story my family was engaged in mission work at Red Lake, Ontario.

Their account of the outpouring of the Holy Spirit upon the staff and students at Loman intrigued us very much because we knew many of the people involved. We were deeply impressed by their conviction that this was a genuine work of the Holy Spirit. Yet from other things we heard about that incident we were convinced that not all was well. The whole episode left me with a distinct fear of speaking in tongues.

At the same time that we heard of God's Spirit working in that Bible school we were involved in some traumatic experiences in our interpersonal relations. All of this led

---

Harvey and Miriam Graber both were born and reared in Old Order Amish families. They met while in Voluntary Service under the Northern Light Gospel Mission in Minnesota. From 1956 to 1961 they were missionaries to the Ojibway Indians at Red Lake, Ontario. Since 1967 they have been engaged in mission work in southern Brazil.

me to some anguished soul searching. "Why, Oh, God, is this confusion and pain thrust upon me?" I asked. I was searching earnestly for answers from God.

Revelations from God

Eventually a word from the Lord came to me in John 14:15-24. The basic message of that passage is, "If you love me" (v. 15) the results will be: (1) "you will keep my commandments" (v. 15) and (2) "I will pray the Father, and he will give you another Counselor, to be with you for ever" (v. 16). On that condition of love which manifests itself in obedience, Jesus says, "I will love him" (v. 21) and "my Father will love him, and we will come to him and make our home with him" (v. 23).

The reality of God speaking to me through this Scripture was dramatic. It was as distinct as sight breaking in upon a blind man. The condition of God for Him to bless me was just to love Him. I thought I already loved Him. I resolved with all my heart to love Him more.

Soon after this divine blessing of insight I had another experience that influenced me profoundly. A group of us went caroling. As we were singing "Silent Night" in the hall of a miners' dormitory, I became lost in the worshipful mood of that song. Chills went up and down my spine and the hair of my body acted like metal in a magnetic field. Then a momentary vision of Jesus appeared to me, perhaps as a confirmation of my resolve to love Him more. I shall never forget the sacredness of that holy vision.

On to Seminary and Mission Field

Gradually I lost my fear of speaking in tongues and

actually began to desire the experience. But I felt it would be wrong to seek to speak in tongues. That would be making an end of the experience itself. I wanted tongues to happen to me as a side effect, very much like my ecstatic experience of worship.

Because of my reticence and mistaken desires, twelve more years passed without my experiencing the gift of tongues. I frequently felt these ecstatic chills of worship while I was singing some favorite hymn, but tongues never overpowered me.

In 1961 we returned to Goshen so I could complete my seminary studies. I also pastored a church on a part-time basis for five years.

In 1967 my family and I went to south Brazil as missionaries. Our first term of mission service in Brazil brought with it many strains. Language study was a frustrating necessity. We lived in three different houses which meant frequent packing up and moving. Over it all loomed the uncertainty about where to locate for our second missionary term.

Our Search Intensified

I was crying for resources to weather such stormy seas when we were given our first three-month furlough beginning in December of 1970. I took my furlough time to investigate more seriously what the charismatic movement had to offer me. Miriam and I attended a fellowship meeting in Vic Hildebrand's basement. Miriam had experienced an infilling of divine love about a year before this. It had such an influence on her that her father even commented on the difference in her.

Our experience together in this charismatic fellowship

generated in us a fresh expectation for a deeper life. We
began asking God for the baptism or infilling of the Holy
Spirit (the terms were not important). For the first time
we asked specifically for the gift of speaking in tongues
as a sign of the Holy Spirit's coming.

On one of those evenings we stayed after the meeting
for prayer. I was praying and asking God to bless me with
His miraculous sign of tongues. One of the brethren
interrupted me to explain that I would have to use my
vocal cords to produce sound. I would not speak in
tongues without my active cooperation. When Peter
walked on the water, no miracle was involved in his walking. That was natural. The miracle was that he didn't
sink. So the operation of my vocal cords would not be a
miracle. Only I must trust the Holy Spirit to guide me in
what sounds would be produced.

That was new and contrary to what I had believed for
years! Soon in a fumbling, uncertain fashion Miriam and
I were speaking in tongues. As we drove home in silence
we felt, on the one hand, a warm inner peace. On the
other hand, the natural man was asking questions: "Was
I really speaking in tongues or was that just me? What
did Peter feel as he walked on the water? His action or
God's?"

Perhaps God in His great love saw that my uncertain
faith needed reassurance. During that night I awoke feeling, as it were, waves of magnetic force passing through
my body. My first impulse was to get out of bed and fall
upon my knees. But I hesitated. What if my moving
around might interfere with what was happening? So I
praised and adored God there in the darkness of my
bedroom without moving.

The following evening I accompanied Nelson and Ada Litwiller to the Notre Dame charismatic Catholic fellowship. On the way home, I shared with them my doubts about speaking in tongues. "Could it be the real thing if my volitional muscles were so involved in producing it?" I asked. He prayed for me and reassured me that night. That encouragement from this highly respected former missionary gave me courage to continue exercising my fledgling gift.

I began the pattern of praying in tongues as part of my private devotional life. But Miriam never again spoke in tongues. She did feel a growing awareness, however, of the presence of the Holy Spirit and of her dependence on Him.

Joy Overflows

The joy that now entered my life was like morning dew. I had not experienced such joy and such an awareness of God's presence since the early months after my conversion at age 19. I soon discovered, however, that such blessedness was the result of being "in the Spirit." My walking in the Spirit was indeed much like Peter's walking on the water. The necessity of disciplining my thought life to maintain the fellowship of the Spirit was essential to maintaining that walk.

What happened to my reading of the New Testament? I can describe it best by using a simile. Suppose a race of nearly blind people had studied art for years. Then one day their sight is restored and they can see colors like we do. Before, they could distinguish only shades of black and white. They would have only a small perception of what artists are painting. But once they could really see colors, they could see those same pictures through new eyes. What a profound change it would make in their perception! So I now see the biblical references to the Holy Spirit with a new understanding. I am especially impressed with how joy, which I now feel, is related to the Holy Spirit.

I have meditated much theologically about my experience and what I found in Scripture. Now I can no longer avoid the obvious. The epistles were written with the assumption that every truly born-again believer knew from personal experience what it was to be in the Spirit.

The joy I felt in the early months after my conversion was the same joy I found again in 1971. For numerous reasons I had bottled up the Holy Spirit. But I was not able to reckon with the creativity and spontaneity of the Holy Spirit. I had never heard God laugh. I had not perceived that joy demands expression and that traditional, formal worship is hardly an adequate vehicle to communicate the exuberant joy of the Holy Spirit. Not until after the bottle broke open in 1971 did I see these dimensions of the life in the Spirit.

Teachers Become Learners

As missionaries we had the good fortune of leading a small, young congregation of humble folk who were emotionally warmer than we Americans are. They were eager learners, but slow. Or was I the slow learner and the poor teacher? I had to learn how to lead a congregation to worship in the Spirit, that is, with the joy and freedom and spontaneity of the Spirit.

I often had to restrain noisemakers, those who thought Jacob's ladder was constructed out of decibels. "You can't sing right until you feel what you are singing," I would tell them. There were times when I almost gave up. Then several members, at different times and in different circumstances, experienced a baptism or infilling of the Spirit. The sign for them, however, was usually uncontrollable weeping rather than tongues. How we needed such worshipers! Again and again, God led us into vital congregational worship experiences. We knew that we personally needed the experience of that quality of worship with others to maintain our walk in the Spirit.

There is a big difference between the "normal" prayer time of praise and thanksgiving and one in which praise and thanksgiving flow forth with tears of joy. But, praise the Lord, that has become a rather frequent experience for our congregation. Emotional? Certainly. Love is an emotion. John 14:15-24 tells us it is on the strength and authenticity of that emotion that Jesus reveals Himself to us and makes His home with us. We are taught to love God with all our strength, soul, and mind (Luke 10:27).

Speaking in tongues is not a highly emotional experience for me. I am so much like a child in the early stages of learning to talk that it is rather humiliating to speak in tongues. But the speaking in tongues that I do practice has helped me to feel a more childlike relationship of trust and dependence upon God.

The really supreme benefits of the baptism are: (1) the sense of His joyous presence—sometimes almost a rippling-laughter joyousness; (2) a greater warmth of personality growing out of the sense of His love for me which, in turn, gives me a greater capacity to love others; and (3) a distinct sense of blessing and a greater power for ministry to the extent the Spirit's role is recognized.

21
A BUBBLE OF JOY

Lowell and Alice Hershberger

Lowell Shares

Was it really mere chance that I read in the *Saturday Evening Post* about the charismatic movement? Through it for the first time I began to comprehend what was meant by speaking in tongues. There Pentecostals told how and why they considered tongues to be of value in their Christian experience.

That speaking in tongues had value as a private prayer language for praise, thanksgiving, and edification was new to me. I thought if this is true, it certainly would be of great value. So I looked up and read 1 Corinthians 14, a portion of my Bible neglected and disparaged until now. I found "He that speaketh in an unknown tongue edifieth himself. . . ." I found that Paul used tongues for praying, singing, blessing, and giving of thanks. Yes, I wanted this despised gift!

Lowell and Alice Hershberger, Scottdale, Pennsylvania, have been employed for many years at Mennonite Publishing House. Lowell works in the bindery and Alice edited *Story Friends*, a weekly periodical for young children. In spring of 1976 Alice began a long and painful bout with cancer which resulted in her death in March, 1977.

God Has Been Changing Me

At the first opportunity I attended a Sunday evening service at the local Assemblies of God church where I hoped to hear a public message in tongues. I was not disappointed. It was beautiful. The interpretation sounded like something out of Isaiah. I wanted this experience of the Holy Spirit and became open to having hands laid on me for this baptism that Jesus as the Baptizer gives to all who ask as promised in John 1:33, 7:37-39, and Luke 11:9-13.

Sometime later, Alice and I were in Chicago for a few days. A brother-in-law of mine took us to Grace Chapel on the North Side where his prayer group were converting Mayflower Gardens, a former beer garden, into a place of worship. At their Sunday morning service we were impressed by the joy and happiness on the faces of those present. We marveled at how quickly time passed. Yet there seemed to be no pressure of time. And the last part of the meeting was the icing on the cake. When opportunity was given for prayer requests, people actually queued up wanting others to pray with them for their own immediate needs.

In the evening service a group of preachers laid hands on me and prayed that I would receive the baptism of the Holy Spirit. Not much seemed to happen. I did not speak in tongues. But I was touched by God. Since that evening He has been changing me in profound ways.

For a short time after this I met in a small house prayer meeting with other Mennonites here at Scottdale, Pennsylvania, who were interested in growing in the Spirit. We listened to taped testimonies given at Full Gospel Business Men's meetings, and within the year es-

tablished the Pittsburgh chapter of the FGBMFI. In one
of the taped messages God used David Duplessis to open
up Acts 2:4, "And they were all filled with the Holy
Ghost, and began to speak with other tongues, as the
Spirit gave them utterance," so that on the way home
from prayer meeting that night I opened my mouth and
spoke in a tongue that the Spirit gave me. Although God
has never moved me to give a public message in tongues,
this has been a blessed part of my personal devotions
through the years until now.

Since the laying on of hands in Chicago, I have never
been the same. My spiritual life took on a new dimension. Jesus became a live person. Oftentimes when I
prayed, always aloud now, tingles ran up and down my
spine. And the Bible was alive. Now I could hardly lay it
down once I started reading. No matter where I opened
the Word, it spoke to me. Slowly my life began to
change. But listen to Alice as she continues our story.

Alice Shares

When the Lord began opening up His Word in new
ways to Lowell, I was both happy and alarmed. I was
happy because I had always wished he would take a
greater interest in spiritual things. I was alarmed because
I was afraid of this "new" teaching about the Holy Spirit
and where it might lead Lowell (and me!). I begged the
Lord to show us if we were being led into some false way.

Lowell invited me to the newly formed Full Gospel
Business Men's Fellowship meetings. I went partly out of
curiosity, partly for a night out, and partly because of the
scriptural injunction, "Wives, be submissive to your husbands" (1 Peter 3:1).

I began to read the FGBMFI magazine, *Voice*. How hungry the articles and stories, plus all that I was hearing and seeing, made me. I pored over Acts and the four Gospels' promises of the baptism of the Holy Spirit. I pondered what Jesus said of His work in John 14—17, and Paul's explanations in 1 Corinthians 12—14.

From my first contacts with Holy Spirit baptized people I was impressed with their joy and how they delighted in talking of Jesus. They also believed God meant it when He said, "If you ask anything in my name I will do it." No ifs or buts about it.

The Valley of Baca Dryness

Hunger for reality in my Christian life deepened. At a tender age I had accepted Jesus as my Savior. I knew I was a child of God. His Word said so.

Through the years I had often made recommitments to the Lord as fully as I knew how. From my early teen years, I had risen early with few exceptions to have a quiet time with the Lord, reading His Word and devotional literature and seeking His guidance. After marriage, I often prayed for love and wisdom in our family relationships. Faithfully I attended prayer meetings and even joined a women's ecumenical study group searching for a closer walk with God.

But the gulf between the love standards of God and my feelings and conduct in our home had deepened. In my growing frustration over my spiritual impotence I grew to hate myself and my husband and our children and every child on our street. The realization came as a horrible shock.

Where was Reality? I felt like a shell with nothing inside—a hypocrite, a Pharisee! How could I as God's child, trying so hard to follow Him, fail so utterly? Where was He?

He had promised that living waters would flow from our innermost being. Where were those rivers? I didn't even sense a trickle! And why wasn't there any joy? Why, too, was it so hard to mention the Lord Jesus in any conversation even with another Christian? And why didn't prayer ever seem to make any difference?

As thirst and longing for Reality grew almost unbearable, I began going forward at every Chapter meeting seeking Jesus' Holy Spirit baptism. For a long time I thought nothing was happening. Now, looking back, I realize my passionate searching was really opening the way through untold layers of religiosity to the core where the real me lived. I was hearing my Father speak and I knew it was His voice, a quiet, inner voice, definitely not of my own fabrication.

Through the years I have often experienced times of depression. These became increasingly dark after I married and became a stepmother to three beautiful, healthy, intelligent, normal children, and even more so after I bore my own child. The wee hours of the night were especially black and filled with hopeless thoughts. But early one morning after an especially debilitating bout with flu (from which I wished I'd never recover), as I was only half awake, I imagined myself entering the curtained room described in *The Listener*, a novel I had recently read. I asked my questions about life, then waited for the Listener (hidden behind the curtain) to answer. Instantly, as the curtains rushed aside, Jesus spoke, "Turn around and face life."

Spiritual Awareness Breaks In

I was wide awake immediately! I knew I had not made up that answer! Months, or maybe several years, later God confirmed that word through three prophetic Bible promises He gave me through Dick Mills. They all emphasized that forward look!

There came a time in my search when God seemed to ask, "How much do you love Me? More than your church? Would you even leave it if I asked you to?

Stunned, I suddenly saw the Mennonite denomination as my idol. How I struggled over that. My church was my whole life. Family, friends, job, recreation, beliefs (except for this teaching on the baptism Jesus promised!)— the roots and tentacles were so deeply intertwined that I couldn't imagine such a step of faith. What would I have left? And my heavenly Father gently answered, "Me."

Praise the Lord! So far He has not called me out of my church family, but, amazingly, has given me a greater love for Mennonites and our Anabaptist understanding of His Word. I praise Him for our rich biblical heritage and strong teaching concerning discipleship and obedience. It provides a stability often missing in other denominations.

One autumn at a weekend FGBMFI rally in our area, I attended the early morning prayer and praise service preceding the Saturday breakfast meeting. As we sang and praised with arms uplifted, my tears began to flow and they wouldn't stop.

People all over the room were praying and praising God in English and in tongues, some ministering to one another. I remember the leader looking at me and saying, "The Lord is sure blessing you."

All I knew was that I couldn't stop the tears and I really didn't care. Jesus loved me! He loved all of us!

Afterward as I walked into the breakfast room I felt surrounded by a sweetness like honey. Or was it a softness like velvet? I couldn't really describe it. And I was so happy! More recently (summer, 1975) I suddenly saw the right description in Psalm 23:5b, "Thou anointest my head with oil; my cup runneth over." That is what happened to me!

Deep in my interior citadel I knew that I knew that I KNEW I was truly God's child and He really truly loved me! For years my mind had assented to the fact, but now I KNEW it, indescribably. That knowing has been a bubble of joy deep within ever since. Guilt feelings are gone. Now there is only a great joy. "How marvelous, how wonderful, is my Savior's love for me."

When did I start praying in tongues? I don't know. Suddenly it seemed very easy to "make up" funny words. I'd do it all kinds of times and places (not so anyone could hear, however), but always just briefly. Then I'd try to figure out, "Is it a language? Or am I just putting sounds and syllables together?" But there were English sounds missing. For example, I could never make an "f" sound even when I tried to put it in.

Never was there any great feeling as a result of worshiping in tongues. Rather, for me, I'd be so lifted up in joy and wonder as I looked at Jesus Christ and loved Him that I'd begin praying and worshiping in my "funny" words. Then my mind watched the words and—thump!—feeling left. Perhaps it is because God permits no rival on His throne. Tongues, however, have been increasingly an avenue of expression for the Holy Spirit

in me to communicate with the Spirit of God. It frees
Him to move in and through my life in ways He chooses.

Praise God He's Changing Me—And Others

One convincing evidence of the validity of the Holy
Spirit baptism has been the change in Lowell.

For years I wondered, "Can't men ever admit they
might be wrong? If just once this man I married would
say, 'I'm sorry,' or 'I was mistaken,' I think I could bear it
to be the one who apologizes first."

The day came! And astonishingly it took all the wind
out of my sails. (Believe me, they were ballooning full of
the wind of self-righteousness.) Suddenly, with startling
clarity, I saw that Lowell was only partly to blame for our
sharp disagreements. In fact, I was maybe more at fault
than he!

Other changes appeared. He became an avid Bible
reader. He began to give not only tithes but also offerings—with joy. He talked faith in the Lord instead of
doubt, health instead of sickness, trust instead of fear,
success instead of defeat. He became more patient and
understanding.

But the baptism of the Holy Spirit is not a door into
human perfection, I discovered. It is no insulation from
the possibility of sinning. One is always a free moral
agent. God's power is available, but I must choose to
avail myself of His presence in me.

In my own struggles with a sharp tongue, a trigger
temper, and widely fluctuating moods the Holy Spirit
has proved His promises over and over. "God is faithful,
who will not suffer you to be tempted above that ye are
able . . . to bear it."

After that special prayer and praise service when God anointed my head with oil and my cup ran over with joy, my emotional climate changed. A sleepless night now offers opportunity for worship, for intercession. Not that I never swing into troughs of darkness, sometimes even months in duration, but there is a difference. Now I know Jesus Christ is with me and in me whether I feel like it or not. Underneath the dark, the blahs, the cold dead mood is that bubble of joy, that knowing beyond any doubt or fear—I am His!

Many more things could be shared, but for me the primary proof that the baptism of the Holy Spirit is valid, scriptural, genuine for me has been His fruit of joy and peace in my life. It has opened the door into a new relationship with my Lord and with people. I wouldn't go back to the other side of that door for anything in all the world. Without the Lord Jesus Christ I'd be nothing. Forgetting those things which are behind, I reach forth to those things which are before (see Philippians 3:13-14).

22

TRIED IN THE FIRE AND PURIFIED

Roy Kreider

My Vision of Renewal

One evening in Israel, while listening to a live concert in a small assembly hall, a graphic scene came suddenly into my view. Before me I saw the broad expanse of the Negev Desert, its thirsting sands, parched gravel, and bald rocks glistening in the fierce summer sun. A deep, dry wadi yawned to the left, stretching toward a lifeless plain. My attention was riveted to the embankment before me, which as I watched began to heave and churn as by some powerful action beneath it. The sands soon turned dark and became muddy; as the mud-swirl thickened, it suddenly tumbled over the side into the wadi as a swelling mud-flow. When the muddiness cleared away a strong fountain bubbled forth, rising into an artesian well. Sweeping mud before it, the rising torrent quickly filled the wadi with clear water flowing strongly toward the dry plain beyond.

With the muddiness gone, a remarkable transforma-

Roy and Florence Kreider live in Tel Aviv and have been Mennonite missionaries in Israel since 1953. They have studied extensively at Hebrew University. During their last two terms in Israel, Roy has been chairman of the Christian Council of Israel.

tion occurred. The banks of the wadi broke out with
greenery. The plain beyond, as by a miracle, became an
orchard of fruit-bearing trees. Among the trees, dressed
in heavenly blue and moving with great energy and joy,
the fruit gatherer was selecting ripened fruit.

My vision revealed a process that was already unfolding. When the thirst had reached a point of desperation,
the fountain had broken out. The movement in that
enormous amount of mud was itself a sign of new begin-
nings through a process of cleansing. Only when the pure
stream came forth did the landscape change and the
fruitfulness appear. the action of the mud was impressive
but my attention was drawn even more to the power that
caused the action. The churning of the mud was only the
prelude to the fountain bursting into full view. The
transformation and fruitfulness of the desert was a
miracle of divine power, a joyful work of the Lord.

I recognized the vision as a parable of my own
experience. The Lord has dealt gently with me—drawing
me to Himself, gradually unfolding me, and enabling me
to follow step by step as He leads me on. I have not
experienced the Holy Spirit through startling manifestations or a sudden invasion of my life. He has never
crashed into my consciousness in a dramatic manner.
Rather, in a beautiful way He enlarges what He has
earlier given to me. From regeneration onward, I have
known the Holy Spirit as He draws, encourages, convicts,
and constrains me. He is always leading me closer to the
Father, and deeper into the full-orbed life of Jesus.

Not Dramatic but Gradual
My discovery of new dimensions in the deep permea-

tion of my life by the Holy Spirit was a gradual process. Already as a student at Eastern Mennonite College, the Holy Spirit was giving me a deeper awareness of the ways of God. The weekly sharing in the prayer circle in the Upper Room still stands as one of the most formative experiences of my spiritual growth through prayer and commitment to Jesus as Lord. The role of the Spirit in that process was very real. He guided me in my preparation for service. He led me to my lifelong partner, Florence. He confirmed our inward call together to an assignment with the church in Israel.

More awaited us in fulfilling that commission than we ever imagined. I clearly recall the deepest desire of my heart. Florence and I prayed together that in the process of our serving the Lord He would lead us ever deeper into His love. We wanted to know more intimately the fullness of the Son through a deepening experience of the life and power of the Holy Spirit in our lives and ministry.

Though the Lord had many things to show me, I do not recall any period in my Christian pilgrimage when I was closed to the divine ministry of the Holy Spirit. My own reading of the Book of Acts left me unconvinced by those who argued that the Spirit manifestations at Pentecost and in the house of Cornelius were exceptional in the ongoing life of the church. I felt then, and I feel now, that God intends us to experience vastly more than the routine level of worship and fellowship with which we tend to be satisfied.

We began to observe this dimension of "much-moreness" upon our arrival in Israel. We soon discovered a few Christians who demonstrated a vitality in their ministry and a reality in their prayers that lifted them into conscious communion with the Father. God was obviously blessing their ministry in a dimension beyond my own experience. The only difference I could put my finger on was the way in which they honored the Holy Spirit and affirmed a conscious experience of a sovereign anointing with the Spirit.

During the next decade Florence and I enjoyed a genuine Word-centered fellowship. Through that fellowship and the Spirit's own illumination we developed also a deepening thirst for all that was apparently our heritage in Christ. One morning when I was alone in my study voicing the praises of the psalms, I became acutely conscious of the near presence of God. In that holy hour I opened wide the gates of my being and invited the King of glory to flood my life with His Holy Spirit. His Presence became wondrously real. Adoration and worship flowed from my inmost being in words transcending human language. For the first time in my life I was actually "lost in wonder, love, and praise."

That was the beginning of a devotional process that I continued morning by morning. The morning was indeed God's chosen hour for granting favors, as the psalms make clear. What I was experiencing was nothing ecstatic, only that the deep within me was communing with the deep that is in God. In my worship the Lord was imparting a divine freshness and illumination which was shining through His Word.

Before long I began to share with Florence the new things that I was discovering. She had sensed the change in me and was quick to affirm and encourage me in the changes God was bringing into my life.

A Rude Checkup and Stunted Growth

Soon after this great experience, I decided to share my discoveries with one of our spiritually discerning visitors. I expected Bill to affirm my experience as Florence had done. Instead, he strongly warned me against attempting to manipulate the Lord's timing. He considered my experience of counterfeit anointing. Bill insisted that he knew of no Holy Spirit infilling that had not followed the pattern of Pentecost. What I was describing might be a preparation, he told me, but it was too low-keyed to be an authentic anointing.

His response left me stunned. My experience was in stark contrast to Bill's own dramatic quickening which he described in detail. As a nominal Baptist he had gone one evening to visit a paraplegic friend. In the course of their conversation his friend suddenly asked Bill whether he had ever really committed his life to the lordship of Jesus Christ. Had he ever asked God to fill him with His Holy Spirit? He was embarrassed. On the way home, Bill decided to do just that. He parked his care in the lane under a tree. Then he prayed his first prayer of surrender. He simply requested the infilling of the Holy Spirit. At once the glories of heaven began flooding in. He heard the sound of the wind of the Spirit as wave after wave of cleansing, renewing, refreshing, and infilling swept over him. So dramatic was his release that he broke out in tongues of high praise to God. This event revolutionized his life. Night after night for three weeks he experienced a repeat of his anointing in his parked car under the same tree.

My own testimony seemed too tame in comparison. I decided to say no more to anyone, and to wait for the

Lord to make the next move. That was in 1959. Ten years later I was still waiting and drying up. Those ten long years, with their delicate and difficult administrative assignments and tough challenges, resulted in a thorough clogging of the fountain. A profound dryness settled in. My prayer life became bound, perfunctory, and ineffectual. I knew that God had honored my earlier initiative in faith. I had begun a gradual process of spiritual growth which would have enabled an inward fortification throughout that extraordinarily difficult decade. But I began to realize that I had drawn the wrong conclusion from the caution of my well-meaning friend. I had abandoned my own quest to be filled continuously with the Spirit.

What I had failed to discern was that the New Testament allows for a wide variety of experiences and expressions in the life of the Spirit. There are indeed instances where the Holy Spirit is poured out upon waiting and prepared people. That is one authentic form of the infilling. But the action of the Spirit is also accurately portrayed equally as the welling up of a fountain, the outflow of an inward spring. Our own initiative enables the infilling to be a continuous action. Growth in the life of the spirit results as we walk in the Spirit. The manner of our worship is crucial to our living in the atmosphere of the Spirit.

Each of these expressions of how the Spirit works includes the other. Each results in the same dynamic interaction that releases new powers in praise, in witness, in ministry, and in a new sense of the immediacy of the Lord's presence. Unfortunately, my friend was attempting to stereotype the work of the Spirit in line with his personal experience. My own infilling of the Spirit followed the second pattern.

I concluded that long and difficult decade on the verge of a nervous breakdown. Emotional exhaustion ushered me into a dark night of the soul which persisted for almost two years. In the meantime I continued as a participant in a small circle of sharing in prayer. A process of divine preparation was at work, a sovereign breaking up of the substructures, making each of us in the circle ready for a renewing, transforming touch from the Lord.

Insight and Healing Flow Again

In 1969 a young couple came from New Zealand to spend several weeks of spiritual preparation in Israel in anticipation of an assignment behind the Iron Curtain. While sharing with John and Yvonne one afternoon in our home, my own experience came into focus. Yvonne felt led to describe a phenomenon from her homeland. In one area of the evergreen forests, at a certain stage of maturing, the falling needles cause a chemical reaction on the mineral-rich soil which produces a hard crust. Before long this surface becomes impenetrable to the rains. As the soil becomes dry, trapping the minerals underneath, plant growth is stunted. The remedy is to open the subsoil to fresh air. The sun and rain are able to do their work again and the plants flourish.

The personal lesson in her story was obvious. My responses and attitudes had created an insensitivity to the Holy Spirit which had blocked the fresh things of God from getting through to me. Consequently, the life of the Spirit within was hindered from expressing itself in the fruit and gifts of Spirit. Through the quiet ministry of the laying on of hands and prayer I felt an inward dissolving and fresh exposure to the healing rays of the Sun of Righteousness. Once more I was bathed in His healing light and love and felt His gentle showers falling upon me.

This glorious dissolving of a decade of barrenness resulted in remarkable growth. One afternoon while I was praying, I sensed the nearness of Jesus. He invited me to walk with Him through the Hall of Memory. At once, in what was more like a revelation than a vision, I saw before me a great hallway, a gallery whose walls were lined with life-sized paintings of events which I recognized clearly. The Lord turned to the first painting on my right, which highlighted that difficult project from which I had emerged two years previously emotionally exhausted. I began to question the unfolding of that ordeal when He suddenly stepped up to that large painting and lifted it from the wall. When I looked behind it, I saw a steaming kettle, its dark contents spilling over the side, deeply straining the Hall of Memory. When I realized the damage my own critical attitude was causing, I asked His forgiveness. Then He placed His hand upon that steaming kettle. Immediately it disappeared, and so did the stain, as my memory-wound was drained of its poison and healed. Then He began to explain His purpose in putting me there. He enabled me to see for the first time that I had learned valuable lessons through that exposure. For the very first time I began to thank Him for that whole encounter. He smiled, and turned to the second painting on the opposite side of the hallway. In that way we walked together step by step into a healing that extended to my

earliest recollections. The further we walked, the more His healing light flooded and illumined, and transformed the past with His cleansing and love. Truly He is *Adonai Rofeikha* (I am the Lord who gives you healing).

The beautiful recognition emerging from that experience was the loving manner of His patient gentle probing, as well as the ongoing process of cleansing and healing which resulted from a response in yielding, and the freshness of His infilling.

In this process of our maturing we never truly arrive. Beyond God's vast horizon there's always more for us to experience. the Lord is renewing His body corporately, as we are being perfected together. Through each of His Spirit-energized disciples we are discovering much more of what awaits us because we are being built together into an habitation of God through the Spirit, into a holy temple of the Lord.

Every stone in this living temple is being fire-polished, to enable the light and life of Jesus to set the entire building aglow. This I believe to be the actualization of His promise to purify to Himself His glorious church so that He might present it to Himself with no stain or wrinkle, but holy and without blemish (see Ephesians 5:27).

This preparation heightens the church's anticipation of her Lord's return. It is worthy of note that whenever the Spirit is allowed to do a new work of cleansing and infilling, the prayer-cry of eager anticipation breaks forth, "Even so come, Lord Jesus!"

For this call of the bride the Bridegroom waits, listening at the threshold of eternity. We should welcome every fresh wind of renewal to heighten anticipation and hasten that glorious meeting.

23

WHEN THE LIVING WATER FLOWS

James and Rhoda Sauder

James Shares

"Oh, so you're missionaries to Honduras. That's wonderful! And have you received the baptism in the Spirit?" the glowing woman questioned Rhoda as she gave her hand a friendly squeeze.

Stammering, Rhoda tried to answer affirmatively. "I'm not sure what you mean, but yes, the Holy Spirit indwells me and guides my life." But that question bothered her after church as we drove to the home of folks from Faith Center who had invited us over for refreshments and sharing. Rhoda recalls a pounding heart which warned her that exciting things were in store.

After some sharing about Honduras, the lady asked me if I had received the baptism. (Her husband was quiet but it was clear that he was backing her up.) I answered her, "In the way I understand it, yes. But in the way you

---

James and Rhoda Sauder are missionaries in Honduras. James has developed training courses in Spanish and supervises the training of local church leaders. He was ordained to the ministry at 19 and installed as pastor of the Cambridge Mennonite Church at Chester, Pennsylvania.

understand it, no." I was never impressed with women who push themselves into doctrinal debate and couldn't understand why this friend would make so much of a fine point like the baptism. Both of us felt somewhat suspicious of this lady who had been a Mennonite. (Why did she leave? we wondered.) However, we didn't refuse the two books she pressed into our hands. Our curiosity was aroused by *They Spoke with Other Tongues* and *Face Up with a Miracle*. The question was pushed into our subconscious but the search was on.

How Did We Get into a Situation Like This?

The church had been growing in Honduras, but there always seemed to be so many little hindrances to growth. We wanted to enable the national church leaders to take on more responsibility. I decided that studies on church growth and leadership training at Fuller Seminary would be helpful, so we moved to the Los Angeles area in southern California.

While reading *Church Growth in Latin America*, I noticed that cases of rapid growth were most frequent among Pentecostal type churches. When we heard that a well-known Latin American preacher was to speak in a series of meetings at Faith Center in Glendale, California, we went. (Ordinarily we attended the Mennonite churches in the Los Angeles area. However, since the closest one was an hour's drive away, we sometimes attended other nearby churches in the evening.)

What interesting services! We were moved by the enthusiastic singing, the clapping and raising of hands, an occasional message in tongues with interpretation, two or three offerings, and preaching which touched the heart.

We liked it (the children did too!) and yet we were hesitant about emotionalism. While the rest clapped, I just folded my arms.

One night during those services, we were sitting on the huge balcony of the Faith Center while the large crowd worshiped the Lord in their characteristic way. Rhoda finally managed to raise her hands above her head in praise to the Lord.

"God just seemed to reach down then," said Rhoda. "I felt His presence all over me." It was after that experience that Rhoda really dug into the two books which were given us earlier.

By February 1971, Rhoda was convinced that tongues is a gift of the Spirit for Christians today. "Some of the experiences in *Face Up with a Miracle* really spoke to my hungry spirit," she testifies. "I cried before the Lord as I was reading the book. I identified with the author as I faced up to my own frustrations.

"One day, while all the rest were at school except baby Sammy, I knelt before the Lord in humble repentance. He showed me many areas of sin in my life. But praise God! I found cleansing and pardon. Then I just asked the Holy Spirit to fill me as Christ promised in Luke 11:13. Also I yearned for Him to guide me into all truth and speak through my lips, glorifying Jesus (John 16:13). Soon syllables formed in my mind and I spoke them, first slowly, then more rapidly. I wrote them down so I could prove what God had given me! I was not overwhelmed with emotion at the time, but did deeply rejoice in the sweet presence of God and felt a tremendous desire to share with James."

Since I had a heavy load of classes and wasn't in the

mood for conversation, Rhoda kept quiet and later found it almost impossible to share her experience with me. But God had her dream in tongues several times. She would wake up praising God in songs! Finally when she found the liberty to share with me, a great joy flooded her being such as she had never felt before. Life was exciting in a different way! A new dimension was unfolding before us.

Didn't We Desire the Fullness of the Spirit Before?

For many years we both yearned for God to work with freedom and power in our time. The New Testament is so full of God's power at work. During the Brunk revivals in 1952 things began to happen. Church members confessed sin and reconsecrated their lives to God. George R. Brunk spoke about the Holy Spirit's empowering for service. Rhoda and I both responded to an invitation for those desiring the Holy Spirit's fullness. We weren't even dating at the time, but each of us sensed the significance of this step in our Christian lives. At times we rejoiced in deep spiritual fellowship among school friends or in our congregations. However, we usually did not feel free to express our joy in the Lord in regular church life. Consequently, the living water did not flow freely.

The same thing had happened to us when we accepted Christ in our early teens. I came to know the Lord and His Spirit, but I didn't experience deep spiritual fellowship in the church. Even after services of great blessing in our church the conversation outside among the young people was still about cars, tractors, and girls. Even though I longed for deep, personal fellowship, only rarely did I experience it. I tried to surmount this by

dedicating myself to serve the church through youth
activities, song leading, and helping in Bible schools.

When I was ordained to minister to a mission congregation at the age of nineteen, I would sometimes
sense God's power as I studied the Word or ministered to
others. But much of our work added up to frustrations.
We were certain that God wanted us to evangelize those
of non-Mennonite background. Many difficulties arose
and we felt the Spirit was frequently grieved and didn't
work freely. Gradually we were settling down to pastoring in a routine way to people of Mennonite and Amish
background, but we didn't care to get too comfortable.
We sensed that God might have other plans for us.

Didn't We Find Greater Freedom in Our Mission Work?

Church planting in a different culture presented
many new challenges. In spite of much satanic opposition, many young folks came to the Lord. Soon they
began telling us of the spiritistic beliefs of the people. I
laughed at some of their fantastic (to me, superstitious)
stories, and expected the problem to disappear. But as I
reasoned and chuckled, the believers declined in their
spiritual lives.

I didn't comprehend that my intellectual reasoning
wasn't any match for the occult practices that had been
entrenched for years in the families. College and
seminary training had not prepared me for dealing with
the occult. Vividly I recall how one professor argued that
the language of Jesus in referring to demons was an ac-
commodation to the people of Bible times. Yet, even
with these limitations, the Lord did help us bring several
families to Christ and they have continued faithful.

Perhaps they discovered things in the Word which were hidden to me!

What Makes the Recent Experience of the Spirit So Meaningful?

I was trained to think problems through to a solution. I had the Word and could interpret it and proclaim it with enthusiasm. However, something was hidden from me. Ever since high school days I had felt a tug-of-war between my rational and my spiritual self. Through prayer and Bible study, I was convinced that "the foolishness of God is wiser than the wisdom of this world" but I continued to battle against the onslaughts of rationalism during advanced studies.

A devout missionary anthropologist from Australia helped me. For him, casting out demons wasn't history. It was modern life! My mind began to change. I discovered that what seemed to be theological difficulties were really cultural hang-ups due to my materialistic educational conditioning.

What Finally Triggered the Breakthrough?

Our whole family was excited when we saw a film about church growth in Guayaquil, Ecuador. It pictured a missionary working hard, but with little response. Then he received the baptism in the Spirit and was on fire for the Lord. His own mission board rejected him, but he found support with the Foursquare Church. He began visiting homes, evangelizing on the streets, and holding services in his living room. One day an elderly blind lady was healed as he prayed for her. She began testifying up and down the streets about what God had done and soon people were flocking to the missionary's home. Hundreds found salvation and many received healing. Soon a church building went up and in a few short years a large, witnessing church was firmly established in that community.

During the film I whispered to the rest that I had read about this very church. Our family was deeply touched to hear the Spanish singing, see the joy on the people's faces as they came to the Lord, and observe the tremendous response to the gospel. Hadn't we also worked for years and with little response? I was so moved I decided to respond to any kind of invitation, regardless of what people thought! Rhoda was quite surprised to see her unemotional husband go quickly up the aisle to the altar, with tears streaming down his cheeks, as soon as the lights came on.

I can't fully describe what happened. The tears and the sweat flowed freely! The accumulated inhibitions and bitterness of years of reserved Christianity were giving way like a breaking dam as the powerful flow of the Spirit moved through me! I lost all concern for onlookers. A few kind brethren calmly laid hands on me and quietly prayed. (There was no grabbing, jerking, or manipulating.) The presence of the Lord filled me in a special way and I sensed a great freedom. As I began to praise God, a new dimension of the Spirit opened to me and the sobs gave way to worship.

Earlier whenever I sought to get serious about praising God, I would remember the bitterness I held against some of my co-workers in Honduras. Why did we get into each other's way when we all wanted to do God's work? I usually blamed them. But finally I had written to

these folks and began to take some of the blame. Still I
didn't overflow with praise as I longed to until that night.
Finally, I felt entirely cleansed of those bitter feelings.
What joy!

I discovered that I could praise God in syllables unknown to me. I hesitated. I liked to have my mind ra-
tionally control everything I did. Could I allow my lips to
say something my mind didn't understand? I decided to
permit the Spirit of God to dominate my mind, and I was
free to praise!

That night at home Rhoda and I praised God in the
Spirit at times, and at times with understanding. As this
flow of living water bubbled over, we experienced such a
beautiful oneness of soul and spirit that we didn't want to
sleep for hours! We wanted that fellowship to continue
forever.

What Was the Fruit of a Fuller Dimension in the Spirit?

I now sensed a greater love for the Lord and His work.
I was amazed how natural it was to start conversations on
spiritual matters once I myself was excited about Jesus!
Many people responded positively, and I could feel for
those who didn't. How negative I had been! Now after I
preached, folks often came up to talk and wondered what
had happened to me. I felt a great desire to share. God
graciously gave me a deeper understanding of His Word.
We were concerned about our return to Honduras, but
after the breakthrough I felt confident that God would
lead us. My highest desire was to please Him first and
then my fellowman.

As we traveled to Pennsylvania after my graduation
from Fuller, I sensed a struggle in my spirit. Would the

Lancaster Mennonite churches and mission board reject
me after learning what had happened? But share I must.
At the state border a verse came to me, "I go bound in
the Spirit up to Jerusalem." Glory! I was bound in the
Spirit, but I wasn't bound by man. I experienced peace
and drove on with a lighter heart.

The first Sunday in Pennsylvania I preached from Acts
1 and 2 but did not state clearly all that had happened to
me. Afterward, my daughter's question, "Daddy, why
didn't you tell them you speak in tongues?" caused me to
think. However, some read between the lines and spread
the news that James Sauder has spoken in tongues!
Rhoda was excited because that day in class she saw evidence of the Spirit freely working in our home congregation.

A precious confirmation about our future service in
Honduras came to us one weekend in northern Pennsyl-
vania. A dear "dutchified" farmer kept saying, "Prase
Godt." I knew something was about to happen!

A group of us shared our testimonies and then began
to pray. As we prayed in the Spirit, suddenly, I was conscious that the person next to me, whom I had known
from childhood, was saying some words in Spanish. I
knew she had never learned Spanish! I exclaimed, "I
hear someone praying in Spanish!"

All was quiet. Then a brother said, "James has the interpretation."

Wow! This was all new for me. I prayed, "Lord, I only
understand a few words."

The answer came, "I gave you a few words and you
tremble. If I would give it all to you in Spanish, you
would faint. Tell what you heard." I did, then another

brother gave a glorious, more complete interpretation. It was a message especially for me and our family, telling us to rest in the Lord, and wait upon Him. That unforgettable experience was like being ordained all over again! We all truly felt the sweet presence of the Spirit.

Rhoda Shares

My joy knew no bounds when James received the anointing of the Spirit in California. The Holy Spirit was changing my life too. So many things were happening to make my spirit leap that even typing a 233-page thesis for him was bearable! The Heart to Heart Fellowship which I had started with my neighbor ladies (I began with a trembling heart) was proving a channel for blessing. They opened up, shared problems, and we prayed about them and saw results. I had just read, *A New Song.* When I told a neighbor about Pat Boone's huge debt and how God had answered prayer, she surprised me by confirming, "Oh, yes, my husband works at the bank where he owed the money!" My faith was strengthened. God is still performing miracles today. I was also writing to a number of prisoners. As I shared with them the marvels of Jesus' working today, light from heaven brightened their cells.

Never in my life had I felt such a burning desire to tell others of Jesus and of all He meant to me. Yes, I had witnessed before, but more out of obligation than out of burning passion. Now I could not keep silent. All glory to Jesus! I wanted to get on the roof and shout so that everyone could hear, "Repent, for Jesus is coming soon!" I felt a tender love for others which I had never experienced before, even for those who differed with me.

A fresh hunger for God's Word made sleepiness much less of a problem during my quiet times with God. And at prayer meetings I would audibly confirm another's prayer. This kept me alert and "with it." It was no small miracle for me to be at peace with myself and God in earth-shaking California! James and I had many opportunities to share our trust in God with neighbors and friends during those months of hundreds of afterquakes following the big shake of February 9.

Once at an ordination at Angelus Temple I saw men fall to the floor as if in a trance and that bothered me. Was this truly of God? I claimed John 7:17. I wanted to know of the doctrine. As I pondered, someone gave me the book, *God's Visitation to the Mennonites* and then it seemed it could be possible. However, I doubted and questioned other things I saw people do who seemed to be filled with the Spirit.

I was becoming critical and cold. Sometimes, especially after beautiful fellowship, prayer, and praise meetings, James would keep me awake for hours. I am a light sleeper, and he would break out in praise to God (often in tongues) while he slept. I didn't want to awaken him, but finally, after many nights of little sleep, I did tell him to please let me get some sleep! He was surprised to learn that his spirit was praising God even as he slept. But I felt condemned for cutting off that avenue of praise. I knew the Spirit was grieved, and I begged for pardon.

Then one night in a dream, I vividly saw Christ. With outstretched arms He looked at me with tender compassion. Such love radiated from His eyes. The wounds on His hands were plain to see. I felt so unclean—so full of criticism, false pride, rebellion, impatience, and other sins of the spirit. I cringed under Christ's gaze of steadfast love. My head fell in shame and I dropped to my knees with my face to the ground. There I lay in total repentance and submission to Jesus, my loving Savior, and felt the power of His blood cleansing me again. My tears turned at last to laughter and as I rose from the ground I at last understood how one could be so overpowered by the presence of Jesus that one would fall to the floor. When I awoke, the interpretation of the dream was clear to me. I must not judge what others do, but just lovingly obey Jesus myself! Praise His name.

James and I never cease to marvel that while we were being blessed in the States, simultaneously God was pouring out His Spirit upon the churches in Central America. No one person was instrumental in this. It was the hand of God. There has been tense opposition at times, but the Lord breaks through afresh.

We returned to Honduras in 1972 with renewed vision and found a different spiritual climate and expectancy than when we had left on furlough. Certainly, we had changed more than anyone! It was so refreshing to witness various gifts of the Spirit being used to bring reconciliation and nurture to the growing church.

Recently, the Lord has opened our blinded eyes to see the need of the ministry of liberation. Several of us missionaries agreed that we could have handled many earlier problems more effectively if we had only exercised the ministry of casting out evil spirits. When the Lord prepares a people for church growth, He equips them with spiritual gifts to gather in the harvest.

Back in Pennsylvania on furlough again, we find much of the initial opposition is over. It has been a real inspiration to us to share in many congregations of Lancaster Conference about the renewal which God has brought into our lives and the lives of others. There is a tendency for some who have experienced the fresh moving of the Spirit to want to leave their group and start a new one where everyone has a similar experience. However, we have found an open door for sharing what we have found in many fellowship groups, revival meetings, and conferences. To us this is a confirmation that God has led us to work for renewal within the Mennonite Church.

The Spirit is continually reaching more church leaders and we can share openly. The Lord is building a bridge of fellowship between the younger overseas churches and the renewal groups in the United States and Canada. We are one in the Spirit. Praise His name!

<h1 style="text-align:center">24</h1>

SETTING THE CAPTIVE FREE
Becky Bontrager

It's the Real Thing

"Wow," I heard myself saying in amazement, completely forgetting where I was and oblivious to the fact that everyone heard me.

"This is real! This is different! This is what I am looking for," I thought.

As one after another of our church young people told how God had touched their lives, my surprise mounted. Hadn't we been praying for revival? So why should I be surprised that it came to our young people?

But wait! Leonard Roth, our youth leader, had the microphone and was giving his affirmation to the events of the previous weekend. He was telling how God had touched him. "I have always hated giving my testimony in public," he said, "because I get emotional and have to

Becky and John Bontrager live at Alden, New York, where John is a contractor and land developer. They are members of the Alden Mennonite Church. Becky is president of the Women's Aglow Fellowship in the Buffalo area and is involved in a prison ministry at Attica State Penitentiary. She shares in the work of the Trinity Christian Counseling Center in the heart of Buffalo and assists with the weekly Bible class at the Potter's Clay Coffee House in Alden.

cry. But I want you to know these tears are for Jesus, and tonight I'm not ashamed of them." This tall, handsome, middle-aged man was talking about Jesus in a refreshingly childlike way that was new to all of us.

This had to be God at work. Not only were the young people different, but God had also touched the Mennonite Youth Fellowship (MYF) leaders. They said they had received the baptism in the Holy Spirit. Our MYF group had returned home from their retreat excited and spiritually turned on. That the Holy Spirit had come upon them in a new way was obvious by the joy and energy with which they shared their testimonies. This was Monday night at the Elma, New York, town park in the summer of 1970.

Saved and Healed

I thought back over my own Christian life. I had accepted Christ as a child during a revival meeting in the Mennonite Church. I went through years of frustration before I realized the peace of God and the assurance of salvation. Then an evangelist came to our church and told it "like it is." He said, "You can't live the Christian life. Jesus will live the Christian life in you if you surrender your life to Him." His main theme seemed to be, "Let go and let God."

At that time I was the mother of two little girls, but I went to each of those meetings because I had such a yearning to yield my life to Jesus and let Him live His life in me. Sometime during that week I gave myself unreservedly to Jesus. As I began to read God's Word and see all His provision for me, I got excited about the possibilities for me as a child of God.

One night soon after this spiritual awakening I was talking to God while waiting in bed for sleep to come. I had a terrible sore throat and every swallow hurt me. Yet that little bedroom seemed literally full of the presence of God. It suddenly occurred to me that He could heal me of my sore throat if I asked Him. The persistence of this truth became so strong, so heavy upon me, that I finally could suppress it no longer. I blurted out, "Okay, God, do it. Heal my sore throat."

I swallowed again to test what God had done. My throat didn't hurt anymore! I knew I had experienced divine healing. I became excited and began to feel strange. It seemed as if my spirit had outgrown my body. The reality of the bedroom seemed to fade, and the reality of the Spirit of God enveloped me. The sensation was so precious I never wanted it to end. I had heard of Pentecostals and "Holy Rollers." But I didn't associate these with my experience because I had only heard of them in disrespect.

I tried once to share this experience with the larger church body but soon realized it was a mistake. I was misunderstood. How could I expect anyone to understand it when I didn't understand it myself?

Later I had a similar experience, this time in a public church service. The sermon stirred my spirit to such depths and God's presence was so real that I remember thinking, "If it weren't for my body holding me down, I'd soar away and be with God." The next thing I knew, the baby I was holding, our third child, was slipping from my arms and my body became limp. My husband took the baby and began fanning me. I was completely conscious, only physically languid. I was more aware of the

Spirit of God than of my surroundings.

Again I didn't know how to explain what had happened to me, but I knew it was of God. I knew I had been blessed in a beautiful way so I kept all these things in my heart and pondered them.

Into the Depths

The family continued to grow. The responsibilities of home, church, and community weighed heavily on me and I began to feel sorry for myself. I was trying to do too much and often neglected my Bible reading and prayer. Jesus said, "The cares of this world and the deceitfulness of riches choke the Word and we become unfruitful." I began to have more times of defeat in my Christian life than victory. Sometimes I repented, but soon I slipped back into the same old rut again.

By now I was mothering five small children, approaching middle age, and feeling like a failure because I could not cope with all the demands. My Christian life was largely unproductive. I felt like a terrible wife and mother. Since I had been so close to God at one time, I also experienced much guilt.

My husband, Johnny, was a successful businessman. He had a cheerful personality and a positive outlook on life. He loved people, and he enjoyed entertaining. He planned large family potlucks and parties and expected me to host them in our home. He often invited business patrons or associates and their families to dinner. He was on many church boards and committees because of his administrative ability and his love for the church. He also served on many civic boards and committees. We sponsored several European trainees and one German refugee family. Because he was president of the board of the Alden Christian School for many years, teachers sometimes boarded in our home and school board meetings were often held there.

Many weeks out of a year John was busy every night with appointments, board meetings, or banquets. I couldn't keep up with all these things so I began to blame my husband for expecting too much of me. I became critical of his business (building contractor and land developer) because it kept him from the children and me. I even began to resent the people with whom he had appointments at night.

Although I had a beautiful house with all the modern conveniences and five healthy, wonderful children, I still pitied myself. We went to church every Sunday. We read Bible stories to the children. We had family devotions some of the time. My husband was generous with money. The children and I did not suffer any financial needs. We lived what folks would call a good, normal, middle-class life. From all appearances I should have been a very happy person.

I had high Christian ideals, but I had forgotten how to let go and let God. I had a longing to be what I could not be. There was a hunger in me that seemed impossible to satisfy, and I began struggling with increased depression. In desperation my husband bought a lovely little cottage on Rushford Lake, fifty miles south of our home, where I could go to relax and meditate and find healing. He knew I loved the water and thought perhaps this was the answer.

But it was too late. I had given up. I couldn't even read the Bible and pray anymore. I only cried and slept. There

was an anguish in me I could not understand or explain. I
remember thinking this must be what it's like in hell—
this is separation from God. Added to all the problems
was a deep sense of shame. Here I was, a professing
Christian, without the will to live. I prayed to God that I
could die. The frustration of knowing what a Christian
ought to be and the realization of my spiritual barrenness
was a gap too large for me. I prayed and cried my heart
out, but it seemed God did not hear—so I gave up. All
this resulted in a nervous breakdown and a period of hospitalization.

Men of God Helped Me Back

After the shock treatments and my release from the
hospital, a ray of hope came to me one day. I was reading
the story of Nebuchadnezzar in the Book of Daniel. King
Nebuchadnezzar too had lost everything. Obviously
insane, for seven years he lived like an animal in the
fields. Then God raised him up, healed him, and established him again as king of Babylon (Daniel 4:36). My
spirit became stirred, strangely warmed. Was God telling
me that I, too, could be useful again? A spark of faith was
fanned into flame.

I began my search anew. I wanted so much for the
Christian life to be real, to be workable. How could I expect our children to believe if it didn't work for me. I
watched the lives of other Christians. Many seemed to
have the same struggles I had with the same lack of
power. Yet occasionally I met someone really excited
about Jesus. Joy radiated in their lives in a way that I
envied.

One such person was Richard Weaver from Harrisonburg, Virginia. He shared his testimony at Laurelville Mennonite Church Center, Mt. Pleasant, Pennsylvania, while we were there. He talked about the Holy Spirit being a well of deep water deep down inside of us and the need of opening up the faucet. The rivers of living water needed to well up, flow out, and touch others.

I began reading books like *Tell No Man* by Edith Rogers St. Johns, *They Speak with Other Tongues* by John Sherrill, and *The Release of the Spirit* by Watchman Nee. I began asking questions whenever the Holy Spirit was mentioned. I read and reread the Book of Acts. Could it be possible that these evidences of the Spirit's power were still being manifested today?

We had been taught that Pentecostals were fanatics living by emotionalism and depending on experiences instead of living by faith. I thought of them as religious people who didn't do things "decently and in order" as admonished by Paul in 1 Corinthians 14:40.

Now I began to see that I had tried to put God in a box so He couldn't reveal Himself to me. I was limiting God. In January 1968, Richard Weaver spoke at our church on the subject of the Holy Spirit. By now I was eager and expectant. After his message five of us responded to the altar call, including our pastor, Dan Yutzy. We shared our individual needs and prayed for each other. The oldest man in the group was healed of a stomach ulcer that night. He often gave testimony of his healing in the months that followed.

When I heard that Howard Bauman, pastor of the Clarence Center (N.Y.) Mennonite Church had received the baptism, with the evidence of speaking in tongues, I was convinced that God was working in our community. I desired to enter into this experience too. I certainly needed that power in my life.

Later Brother Bauman shared his experience in our church and many, including myself, asked that night for Jesus to baptize us in His Holy Spirit. Although Brother Bauman laid his hands on us and prayed for us to receive the Spirit, there was no visible evidence that our prayers had been heard.

God Had to Overcome My Hang-ups

As I look back, I see that I had many hang-ups and fears that hindered me from receiving the fullness of God through His precious Holy Spirit. I knew I already had the label of being the emotional type. Now since my nervous breakdown, I was very self-conscious about what people might think about me. I didn't want people to say that emotional people were the only ones who were susceptible to the baptism of the Holy Spirit. Had I known that the baptism in the Holy Spirit could be a very private experience between me and God alone and that speaking in tongues also is a private prayer language, I believe I could have received the baptism sooner. I thought that if one spoke in tongues, it was always interpreted in a public meeting and shared with the entire church body. I later learned that the gift of tongues and praying in tongues are two different things.

Consequently, I said to God, "If the gift of tongues ever comes to our church let it come to someone very level-headed and stable." By telling God how to do it, I only hindered my own receiving of the baptism. A lack of faith and understanding, mixed with fear, hindered me.

During Thanksgiving weekend of 1971, Wes Smith spoke at our church. This was the same young man who had been the retreat speaker for our MYF the summer before. He was the person through whom God had worked to reach and change our young people. It was easy to see God had done something dynamic in their lives. I was especially impressed and amazed at my teenage nephew. God had reached down and touched that rebellious, disobedient, seemingly obstinate young man. He was changing him into a submissive, lovable, devoted Christian who was reading and studying the Bible and caring about other people. It didn't wear off.

All my life I had been told I had received the Holy Spirit when I was baptized by water; however, the power of the Spirit was lacking in my life. I was still struggling with depression, bitterness, and self-pity. I hated myself for being so nervous. The medication I was taking helped me but I was not a happy, productive Christian.

Wes Smith wasn't an overly dynamic speaker, yet God used him that Thanksgiving to bring revival to me and to our church. He gave an invitation that night to come to the altar for any need you had in your life. Just as I was thinking that no one would respond, our daughter, Meriul, and our son-in-law, Bruce, walked together to the front of the church. Another couple followed them just before the service closed. These four persons were invited to go to the pastor's study. The rest of us were dismissed and went home.

He Did It! God Baptized Me!
The next afternoon the Spirit of God seemed to descend upon me as I was leaving the church. I had

continued to ask God to baptize me with His Holy Spirit, and now suddenly I knew He was doing it. I was so elated I began to praise God in English the best I knew how. Tears of joy streamed down my face as I drove out of the churchyard. I wondered why I couldn't pray in tongues. God was here in me and all around me and I wanted to bless Him. I wanted to pray in tongues.

I had heard that praying in the Spirit (tongues) edifies oneself and blesses God. I no longer cared what people thought. Some months later while praying with a small group two words came to me. Dan Yutzy encouraged me to say them. "But they sound so stupid," I said.

"Never mind. Just let them come out," he coaxed.

"*Allah baba,*" I said embarrassed.

"Praise God! Hallelujah!" Dan said, as if I had accomplished a marvelous feat.

I couldn't seem to get past those two words. One day all alone in my kitchen I said, "God, I seem to have a hang-up about praying in tongues. Please help me. '*Allah baba*' sounds stupid to me, but if it blesses You, God, I'll say it. I want this gift to be only for Your honor and glory."

At that very moment He opened my mind to understand the meaning of these two words. *Allah* means God in Aramaic and *baba* means daddy (or *abba* as in *abba* father). "God, my Daddy," I cried over and over. "God, my Daddy, I love You! God, my Father, my beautiful wonderful Father. Thank you, thank you, thank you," I said through tears of joy.

I raised my hands and prayed, "*Allah baba, Allah baba,*" and then more unfamiliar words came and I was praying in my own prayer language, a language I didn't understand, but a prayer I knew went straight to God.

Now back to our Thanksgiving weekend with Wes Smith. On Saturday night all the young people from the three area Mennonite churches were invited to our house because we have a large recreation room in our basement. Wes Smith, Dan Yutzy, and Ted Weaver, a Christian pilot who had flown Wes Smith to us in a small private plane, shared more of God's Word and their own testimonies with the young people and with us. Ted Weaver spoke about healing, binding evil spirits, and casting out demons. After this message we were asked to share any prayer requests or needs we might have.

Several of us asked for prayer. Completely forgetting that this meeting was for the MYF, I found myself kneeling in the center of the room in front of Wes Smith, the pilot, and Dan Yutzy. Sitting on the floor around me, from wall to wall, were the young people—beautiful, sympathetic, understanding young people.

I heard myself asking for healing. I told about my medication. I wanted to be free of depression without the use of drugs. They prayed for me, and so did all the young people. I felt one with them and with God.

Many beautiful things happened that night in our basement. Young people rededicated their lives to Jesus and were baptized in His Holy Spirit. There were prophecies and answers to prayer. There was confession of sins and forgiveness. Some couldn't take it and left early, but many were helped that night. On Sunday morning the revival broke out in our church with added fervor and continued throughout the day in private homes and climaxed in the evening meeting.

I was on cloud nine or one hundred and nine! The joy

and the power and the presence of the Lord became so real I could hardly sleep at night. I just wanted to thank Him, praise Him, love Him, and know Him. On Sunday night I decided to quit taking my medication, and I claimed my healing. I accepted it by faith. With Job I said, "Though he slay me, yet will I trust in him" (13:15) and with the three Hebrew children of the fiery furnace, I said, "My God is able to deliver me, but if not, be it known to thee, O Satan, that I will not serve you or go back on the medication." (See Daniel 3:16-18).

It was Sunday night. Our weekend meetings were over. Wes Smith and the pilot returned home, but I and many others would never be the same again. Those rivers of living water were streaming from the depths of my being. Small wonder that I could not sleep that night. I wanted to praise God, to thank Him, to love Him. I had wasted so much time. I had so much to learn.

Into the Wilderness Like Jesus

After the baptism in the Spirit, the peace and joy and love of God so filled me I wanted to share it with everyone. I was so zealous I tried too hard and turned people off. I had not yet learned that "in quietness and in confidence shall be your strength" (Isaiah 30:15). I needed to learn to wait for God to open doors.

Satan began to take notice of me and to work me over. Later I learned that severe temptation follows every great experience with God. Even Jesus, after His baptism in the Jordan when the Holy Spirit came upon Him in the form of a dove, was led into the wilderness to be tempted of the devil. This is necessary to establish and strengthen us.

I too found myself in a wilderness, and it seemed that my temptations were more than I could bear. I began to sink into depression again. "You can't let this happen to me, Lord," I cried. "I have claimed my healing in faith and You must honor Your Word. You said, 'If ye shall ask anything in my name, I will do it!' You can't go back on Your Word."

But I continued to grow worse. The old fears began to return. The joy of the Lord was gone. The planning and responsibility of our oldest daughter's wedding was upon me, and I began to fall apart. Worse still was the spiritual conflict. Had God let me down or was I doing something wrong?

Satan had me in a whirlwind and I felt tossed to and fro like a rubber ball. I went from faith back to doubting and vice versa. In my desperation I said over and over again, "God, what do You want with me?" I almost shouted it at Him. As day after dreary day dragged by with no response, I groaned, "Lord, where do I go from here?"

It would take too long to tell all the details of my temptation experience. Suffice it to say it seemed longer than forty days, and I wasn't a conqueror over Satan as Jesus was. I felt pressured and battered and pushed out of shape until I gave up in defeat. I remember saying to myself, "I can't buck the establishment." So in desperation I went back to the doctor and resumed taking my medication, bitterly thinking, "I'll never again ask God to heal me." The shame I felt was the worst of all.

Our daughter's wedding was beautiful and momentarily I was grateful for the medication. But my spirit was in turmoil, not understanding what had gone wrong.

Spiritually, I was in confusion and anguish. I felt dead inside myself.

I had tasted and seen that the Lord is good. I had touched reality. I had glimpsed eternity. I had seen the hidden treasure and now I must sell all that I have to buy that field. I had fallen in love with Jesus and now I knew I could never live without Him.

"Lord, where do I go from here?" I continued to ask. I was full of self-pity and pride. I knew I could never face all those young people who had heard me ask for healing, now that I had gone back on the medication. I had claimed my healing and I wasn't healed.

Broken, bitter, and empty I fled to a little hotel room about fifty miles from home. But I sensed that God had followed me. "God, why are You here in this room with me? Why are You loving me?" I had gone away in desperation to be alone, not caring who I hurt or what would happen. Yet God's presence was so real I could almost touch Him. So I repeated the question almost insolently, "God, why are You here with me when You know I blew it?"

And God answered. From that moment, He began to bring me out of confusion and into Himself. He reminded me that Abraham, too, had blown it when he had a child, Ishmael, by Hagar. He really messed things up. (The Arabs and Jews are still in conflict.) But God Almighty came through with His promise to Abraham. He still gave him Isaac, child of laughter, child of promise.

"And I will bless you too," God said to me. "I am faithful even when you fail. I can make order out of chaos. I want to bless and heal you spiritually but you are so preoccupied with the flesh, with physical healing, that I can't get through to you." I began to cry as He continued to speak to me. "I want to heal you spiritually. I want to give you your child of promise," He said.

Walking in the Spirit

Oh, what joy and hope began to fill my heart. God hadn't abandoned me after all. He was still going to bless me. He was talking to me! His presence filled the room. "But what about Ishmael?" I asked. "Ishmael can't be unborn?" I was still thinking of my physical healing and the medication. "I can't go home until you tell me about Ishmael," I repeated. "What shall I do about Ishmael?"

"Don't you see?" God answered. "Ishmael represents the flesh and Isaac stands for the Spirit. The flesh and the Spirit are at enmity one with another. Don't you remember that Ishmael was eventually sent away never to torment Isaac again? You must walk after the Spirit and not after the flesh. The flesh must die!"

Suddenly, I saw it. My spiritual eyes were opened and I saw the love and mercy of God. I understood what He was saying and I laughed and cried as I thanked Him. I could hardly contain myself. I felt let out of prison—the prison of myself. I was free—free as a child, free to let God begin His work in me, free to go home. I said with Job, "I have heard of thee by the hearing of the ear: but now mine eye seeth thee" (42:5).

I knew now that I had been taking myself too seriously. My emotional and physical weakness had become an obsession with me. That day was the beginning of walking after the Spirit for me, the beginning of my spiritual maturity. Later I realized that God also had a blessing for Ishmael (the flesh) as well as for Isaac. He would even bless my flesh as I laid it on the altar of God.

I repented of my bitterness and self-pity and went home. I asked my husband and family to forgive me for my selfishness and told them what God had done for me. As I studied His Word, God revealed to me many areas in my life that needed changing. That was painful. It is not easy at 47 to change a lifetime of selfish habits and attitudes. But now I wanted to change. I wanted to be like Jesus, and I knew I had a long way to go. I asked Him to turn up the heat, if necessary, to purify me. I gave Him permission to put me back on the potter's wheel and shape me into the vessel He wanted. I told Him to continue to prune me even though it hurts so I could bring forth fruit, not thirty, not sixty, but a hundredfold.

God heard that prayer. He took me seriously. He began to show me all the rot in me. One Wednesday night at prayer meeting, I asked for prayer. After they prayed for me our pastor looked at me and said, "I believe I have a word from the Lord for you." Imagine my surprise and embarrassment when he told me to read Ephesians 5:22 and 1 Peter 3:1 regarding wives submitting to their husbands. I knew it was a message from God, so I again confessed my rebellion and asked forgiveness.

I had also been praying that God teach me how to humble myself. He began showing me many ways and I made confessions I never would have dreamed I could make. In the weeks that followed I prayed for a deeper love for my husband, so I could truly love, honor, and reverence him with all my heart. I began to see how immature and selfish my love had been.

Slain in the Spirit

In June of 1973 I had the privilege of going with a friend to New York City to a Full Gospel Business Men's convention. For me it was an amazing and wonderful experience. Seeing hundreds of people praising God with uplifted hands, from all denominations, and feeling the presence of the Spirit in such depth is hard to describe.

That week at the convention God answered many of my questions about the work and gifts of the Spirit. Also I learned much about walking in the Spirit. I had many things to unlearn, many misconceptions. God took me all apart and put me back together again.

One night in my hotel room I couldn't sleep because God was talking to me. He began to remind me of all my husband's wonderful qualities and filled my heart with a great love for him. He told me that He had given me my husband—that he was just right for me—handpicked by God. I could hardly wait to go home and ask his forgiveness for all my past criticism and ingratitude. Submission to God and to my husband have been much easier since that night. It's fun when you remember it's "as to the Lord." Love begets love and I have been repaid a thousand times over.

The last night of the convention I was slain in the Spirit. This was after the large meeting was dismissed and many had left or gone to their hotel rooms. Small groups of people had stayed and were praying and singing together as if not wanting the fellowship to end. I couldn't leave that room. I felt compelled to stay. The Spirit of God was there.

I edged up to one small group just to watch and listen. They soon included me. A lovely, middle-aged lady with a radiant face was praying audibly for one person after another. As she put her hands on their heads or shoulders and prayed for them, they crumpled to the floor. I had seen something similar in a Kathryn Kuhlman meeting and I knew it was the power of God.

I watched them as they lay there. Some were soon up on their feet again. Some stayed down a long time. Some raised their hands and praised God with their eyes closed. Some prayed in tongues. Some were perfectly still. Some cried. Some sang. But all were obviously blessed.

The peace and joy they experienced was so evident that I became bold enough to ask one lady to tell me about it. The light on her face was so pronounced I said to her, "You're beautiful!" She quickly responded, "It's Jesus!" I became so unselfconscious that I began picking the fuzz of the rug from her slightly disheveled hair. She was prayed for numerous times and each time she fell to the floor. Each time she stayed longer and looked more beautiful. When she got up she staggered and laughed and was radiant. Again I said, "Tell me about it." Again she laughed and answered, "It's Jesus!" I thought of the Scripture, "Be not drunk with wine . . . but be filled with the Spirit" (Ephesians 5:18) and I wondered if this lady was drunk in the Spirit.

Then the lady who was praying over people looked at me and asked if I too wanted to be blessed. I said "yes" and she put her hands on my shoulders and prayed for me. As I raised up my hands in praise to God, my knees became as water and I fell to the floor. Waves upon waves of love enveloped me. I felt bathed in love, cleansed and beautiful and free. I knew I was on the floor in the big ballroom of the Americana Hotel in New York

City and I didn't care. I was not ashamed or embarrassed. I was glad, glad, glad! I knew God's love in a way I can never explain. Later I began to laugh, laughing like a little child at play. I said, "God, it's good to laugh. I've cried so many tears already." Then I remembered Isaac, child of laughter, and I knew God was keeping His promise to me. And I said to myself, "This must be holy laughter."

Now I knew what had happened to me those many years ago when I had been healed of a sore throat and thought I was dying. I was also reminded of that time at church when I almost dropped the baby. It had happened to Ezekiel, to Paul on the road to Damascus, and to John on the Isle of Patmos. Why should we be surprised if Christians are slain with God's presence in our day?

Jesus is healing me, changing me, making me whole. He is bringing this nervous, insecure, weak person into strength. Through the reading of His Word and through the power of the Holy Spirit He is establishing, strengthening, settling me (1 Peter 5:10).

My testimony in a nutshell is this: "Thou hast turned for me my mourning into dancing: thou hast put off my sackcloth, and girded me with gladness; to the end that my glory may sing praise to thee, and not be silent. O Lord my God, I will give thanks unto thee for ever" (Psalm 30: 11, 12).

Truly He has set this captive free! I shall be forever grateful!

THE EDITORS

Roy and Martha (Horst) Koch, now of Goshen, Indiana, were born at St. Jacobs, Ontario. Roy was pastor of St. Jacobs Mennonite Church for twenty-one years.

He has also served as principal of Ontario Mennonite Bible School (1952-57); pastor of South Union Mennonite Church in West Liberty, Ohio (1957-70); moderator and president of the Ohio and Eastern Mennonite Conference (1962-66 and 1969-71); conference minister of the Indiana-Michigan Mennonite Conference (1971-75); and moderator of his denomination (1963-65).

Martha was office secretary of the Indiana-Michigan Mennonite Conference (1971-75) and since 1976 has worked for Provident Bookstore, Goshen, Indiana. She has spoken at various women's meetings.

Martha graduated from Ontario Mennonite Bible School, attended Goshen College, and graduated from Carter Secretarial School, Elkhart, Indiana. Roy holds degrees from Waterloo College (BA) and Goshen Biblical Seminary (ThB, BD, MDiv).

They are the parents of Robert, Arlene (Mrs. Ken Holdeman), Richard, Rodney, Helen, and Sheila; they have five grandsons.

Since 1975, Roy has been employed as director of Public Relations for Bethany Christian High School, Goshen, Indiana. The Kochs are members of the East Goshen Mennonite Church.